Recommendations

Selah is a book of life's most precious and important relationships. Sharon Rabon addresses these important circles of our life relationships—God, family, friends—with her personal stories and Bible-based practical applications. She is authentic, sincere, practical and wise. The book is a beautiful read for young moms and aging women as well. *Joanne Cox*
Wife of Pastor Emeritus Randy Cox l Beacon Baptist Church l Raleigh, NC

Sharon is a "one-of-a-kind" pastor's wife and friend. Her book reads like having a one-on-one conversation with her. She's the real deal! Thanks, Sharon, for another "helps" book.
Renee Cox
Wife of retired Pastor Jack Cox l Liberty Baptist Church l Durham, NC

I am excited that my friend, Sharon Rabon, has written this devotional book, as all of us need a pause to read and journal our thoughts on God's love. This book will encourage and strengthen your walk with the Lord. *Vicky Mutchler*
Pastor's wife of Mike Mutchler l Grand View Baptist Church l Beavercreek, OR

Sharon uses everyday family life to take biblical principles and really hit home in many areas that we need to just breathe and take in! Do not let the importance of life just pass you by. Take time to ponder. *Amy Sapp*
Helpers of Joy l Faith Music Radio l Conference Speaker

To purchase additional copies of *Selah*,
visit sharonrabon.com

Selah

PAUSE TO PONDER

Sharon Rabon

Pause

Copyright © 2018 by Beacon Publications

All Rights Reserved

Printed in the United States of America

ISBN: 978-0-692-04288-5

Published in 2018 by Beacon Publications, a ministry of Beacon Baptist Church

Beacon Baptist Church

2110 Trawick Road

Raleigh, NC 27604

All Scripture quotations are taken from the King James Version.

Author - Sharon Rabon

Cover Design and Layout - Lucinda Brooks

Editor - Joy Edmonds

The author and editor have researched diligently to give proper credit to quotations
and thoughts that are not original with the authors. It is not our intent to claim origi-
nality with any quote or thought that could not readily be tied to an original source.

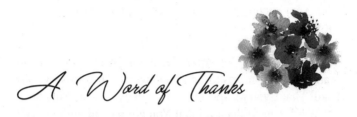

A Word of Thanks

"Thank you" seems inadequate when I consider a few words to say about the people who strongly impact my life.

Thank you, Tim, for continuing to support me as I write. You are my husband, soulmate, leader and pastor. I love you so very much! Apart from being known as a child of God, I only want to be known as the wife of Tim Rabon.

Thank you, my adult kids. I love being mom to you, and I wouldn't be able to do what I do without your continued love and support. Tim and Laura, Philip and Nichole, Chris and Joy, I love you with all my heart! Oh, and thanks for my Cute Kids! I enjoy every moment that I invest in their young lives!

Thank you, Loretta Walker, for helping me with the organization of this book. Your encouragement truly pushes me to keep writing.

Thank you, Joy. Not only are you the best daughter a mom could ask for, you are the most awesome editor ever! What a great combination.

Thank you, Lucinda, for being so easy to work with. Without complaint you make changes just because I want to try something new.

Thank you, Nancy Pauley, for mentoring me. When I was only 18 years old, you willingly taught me so much about being a pastor's wife. Your life was and continues to be an example for me to follow!

Thank you, Beacon ladies, for the love and support that you show to my husband and me. You truly make ministry enjoyable. Your encouragement to me is wind beneath my wings! I love each of you!

Thank you, Jesus, for willingly dying for my sins. I'm so thankful that I'm saved and can live my life to serve the Lord! Thank you for speaking to me daily through Your written Word. I'm so thankful that You are patient with me as I grow in my walk with You!

About the Author

Sharon grew up in a Christian home in Midland City, Alabama. She trusted Christ as her Savior when she was a child and gave her life to serve the Lord in lifetime ministry as a teenager. Sharon married her high school sweetheart, Tim Rabon, July 27, 1979. In 1981, they were asked to join the staff of Beacon Baptist Church in Raleigh, NC. In 1997, her husband became the pastor of that same church. Sharon is director of ladies' ministries, serves as her husband's secretary and speaks at ladies' conferences. She is the mom of two sons and one daughter, all of whom are married and serve in lifetime ministry. She is known as Nana to 7 Cute Kids!

To the Reader

My Friend,

It is with excitement that I bring to you more thoughts from God's Word. I honestly can't believe that I have now written my second devotional book; yet, here it is.

The word *Selah* is used many times in the Old Testament, and especially in the book of Psalms. When I read the word at the end of a Psalm, I always think, "What does God want me to pause to consider or to think about? I entitled the book, *Selah* because it simply means pause to ponder; stop and think. That's what I have done in my quite times with God. I've paused to ponder what God is saying to me. I've simply stopped to think about how the verses I read apply to me today. I challenge you to use the journaling page after each devotion to write what God has spoken to you about that day.

Grow along with me as you read your Bible every day, writing down a few thoughts that you gleaned from God's Word!

From My Heart To Yours,

Sharon

Living Close to the Edge

Psalm 119:4
*"Thou hast commanded us to keep
thy precepts diligently."*

Our family enjoys doing a variety of things together. We enjoy sitting around the table and telling a happening to its fullest. We enjoy going to baseball and amusement parks. We enjoy seeing places of beauty that God has created. We enjoy people. We enjoy fellowship.

However, there are a few things in life that our family doesn't enjoy. We have never enjoyed getting up early on vacation just to go to breakfast. We have never enjoyed horror movies or scary places. We have never enjoyed being too close to the edge of a pond or pool with no railings, especially at night. We loved seeing the Grand Canyon, but we did not enjoy the opportunity of being close to the edge in certain places of that vast hole with no guard rails.

When our children were young, I recall going to Washington D.C. for Thanksgiving holidays. Thanksgiving night we were walking on the sidewalk beside the Reflecting Pool. Tim Jr. was so scared. He cried, "Daddy, don't make me walk close to that water." It was dark, and the water

1

looked very scary to him. Philip, on the other hand, had no fear. We were the ones afraid that if we turned our backs he would be in that dark water.

One thing was for certain: if we taught the children to stay on the sidewalk, a proper distance from the water, neither of them would get hurt no matter their fear or lack of it. It was in the training. We must train our children to keep distance from what could physically harm them.

Many of us tend to the physical needs of our family, including our own selves by staying away from harmful chemicals, wearing life preservers around water, or watching the traffic when on busy streets. The physical care is very important, but what about the spiritual care of our families?

Ask yourself these questions:

1. Are you growing spiritually?
2. Is your spiritual discernment gaining maturity?
3. Do you try to live as close to the edge of the world as possible and still maintain your Christian walk with the Lord?
4. Do you flirt with the world on Monday through Saturday and try to play perfect Christian on Sunday or when you are around your church friends?
5. Do you live close to the edge at work in your speech, dress and actions?
6. Do your children see you with one foot hanging on to worldly ways and the other foot trying to maintain your spiritual life?
7. Do you have the wrong friends, thus setting a wrong example for how your children choose their friends?

Spiritual victory and living the Christian life is only gained through total surrender to the Lord. Many may believe that the cost is too great to give up living close to the edge, but just the opposite is true.

Romans 12:1-2 exhorts, "I beseech you therefore, brethren, by the mercies of God, that ye present your bodies a living sacrifice, holy, acceptable unto God, which is your reasonable service. And be not conformed to this world: but be ye transformed by the renewing of your mind, that ye may prove what is that good, and acceptable, and perfect, will of God."

Ask the Lord to guide you to stop living close to the edge.

Pause to Ponder

Me, Myself and I

I Corinthians 10:24
"Let no man seek his own, but every man another's
wealth."

I love the songs written by Patch the Pirate. We were introduced to his children's songs years ago when our children were toddlers. We began buying those yellow cassette tapes whenever possible. A yellow cassette was definitely a smart marketing move as our children knew if we put a yellow tape in the player or not. Patch the Pirate songs are usually about building Christian character. Songs like "Pigs Don't Live in Houses," "I Love Broccoli," and "Rise and Shine, Lazy, Sleepy Head" are among our favorites. There is one particular tape that stands out in my mind. The title of the cassette was *Kidnapped on I-land.* The story is very captivating even to an adult. A boy was kidnapped by the "sel-fish" and taken to "I-land." The ways of the "sel-fish" were taken by the boy, and he became very selfish as well. His favorite words became "Me first, me first, me first." These were the very words of the "sel-fish" and were said over and over on the cassette.

Tim, Jr. was very young when we purchased this cassette. As he listened to it over and over, he got the message alright. He got the WRONG message. He began saying, "Me first, me first, me first" in his little preschool voice. We obviously had to stop listening to "I-land" until Tim got old enough to understand the RIGHT message.

Likewise, how many times do we choose to get "Kidnapped on I-land"? The only things important to us are the selfish desires that consume us. Selfishness ruins lives, wrecks marriages, and drains the joy from all whom it consumes. We must all choose to control our selfish appetites and desires.

The Bible clearly teaches us to stay away from selfishness. Philippians 2:21 says, "For all seek their own, not the things which are Jesus Christ's." Pleasing self causes division in family and friendships. A selfish person usually becomes very prideful and uncorrectable. This type of person is cold and indifferent toward the correction of the Lord. In order to be used by God, we must remain correctable, teachable and tender toward the ways of God.

Do not allow yourself to live on "I-land," so the "sel-fish" will not affect you!

Pause to Ponder

It's All about Gratitude

Ephesians 5:20
"Giving thanks always for all things unto God and the Father in the name of our Lord Jesus Christ;"

Someone once said, "Gratitude is the attitude that sets the altitude for living."

The words *thank you* are two of the kindest words in the English language. Of course, there are many tones and expressions that can accompany these words. A child is given a piece of candy and the parent says, "Say, thank you." Sometimes the words are said from a heart of stone, and sometimes they are said with kindness. Nonetheless, we all believe that we should train our children to say these kind words.

We often take things for granted. Many of us have had life given to us on a silver platter. The attitude of many parents today is to make sure that their children have more than they had while growing up. While this attitude is meant for good, it is destroying Americans by the dozens. We have lost the gratitude that our grandparents and great grandparents had for the things that they had to work for.

Many times our mindset is that if we don't have material things then we are not blessed. That is simply not true. God's blessings are much more than materialistic gain. The principle of sowing and reaping applies here. If we sow gratitude, we will reap blessing. God's blessings are as innumerable as the sand on the seashore. We must look for them, however. If you are dwelling on the rainy day, you may not see the flowers that the rain caused to bloom. If you are caught up in the storm, you may miss the rainbow that God has supplied. If you are looking through the negative lens of your life, you may miss the people that God has placed in your life to be a blessing to you.

As women, we have so much to be thankful for. Be thankful if you have a husband in your home. Be thankful for the example of the perfect woman laid out for us in Proverbs 31. Be thankful for your children. Be thankful for the people that the Lord has allowed to influence your life for spiritual gain. Be thankful for the Bible. Be thankful for your church.

Gratitude is an attitude. We choose whether to be grateful for what we have or to complain about things that happen around us. Complaining is the negative attitude that usually begins to replace thankfulness. It happens gradually. A complaint here or there adds up to an attitude change after awhile. Just as we would tell our child to stop complaining about what they don't have and to be thankful for what they do have, we should do the same.

Remember the old hymn, "Count your blessings, name them one by one, count your many blessings see what God hath done." Make a list of what you are grateful for. I think you'll see that it is all about gratitude!

Pause to Ponder

_____
_____
_____
_____
_____
_____
_____
_____
_____
_____
_____
_____
_____
_____
_____
_____
_____
_____
_____
_____
_____

Day 4

The Birthday Event

Psalm 143:5
*"I remember the days of old; I meditate
on all thy works; I muse on the work of thy hands."*

Birthdays have always been a big event around the Rabon household. Growing up we had a party for each child every year. One year they could invite a few friends to join the family, and the next year was only family. We always tried to make the family year more special than the friends year so that the children would look forward to the family parties as well. Each year the birthday child would decide what kind of cake they would like. I would do my best to draw that character and decorate the cake accordingly. Gifts were opened, pictures were taken, and games were played according to their liking. Why? Because a birthday is a special event!

As the children grew up and became adults, the birthday tradition has continued. The birthday person chooses the restaurant where the family will eat. Then, we all come home, and the birthday person opens their gifts and cards, and we take pictures. The choice of ice cream cake is served after the candles have been blown out. Why do we continue this tradition? Because a birthday is a special

11

event!

Just like the physical birthday is special, so is the spiritual birthday. My husband calls the pastor who was preaching the night he got saved every year and thanks him for preaching the Gospel clearly that night. When our children were young, we made sure that we regularly talked about their spiritual birthday at family devotions and whenever possible. To this day, it thrills me so much to hear one of our children say, "Today is my spiritual birthday." Our grandchildren, affectionately known as Nana's Cute Kids, celebrate their spiritual birthdays each year with a cupcake and a candle. We even sing to them. Why? Because a spiritual birthday is a special event!

We would all agree that the physical birthday is very important to recognize. Let's also begin to put importance on our spiritual birthdays. Make the physical and spiritual birthdays a big event in the life of your family today!

Pause to Ponder

Day 5

Who Is God to You?

II Samuel 22:3
*"The God of my rock; in him will I trust: he is my shield,
and the horn of my salvation, my high tower, and my
refuge, my saviour; thou savest me from violence."*

Children need parents who are willing to help them
through the trials that come in their lives. A little problem to an adult can be huge to a child. Someone may say
hurtful things to them or about them. They may get left
out when playing on the playground. No one seems to
want them in their circle of friends. These things happen
to our children and we, as their parents, do our best to
hold them and to help them overcome their hurts. That's
what parents do! We are there for our kids no matter their
age. We desire to protect them and to guide them. We do
our best to lift them up with words of encouragement and
praise. When something of this sort happened to one of
our children, it was a habit of mine to take my hand, put it
under their chin, lift their head and say, "Look into Mom's
eyes. Everything is going to be okay."

In Psalm 3, David is running for his life from his own
son, Absalom, and he talks to God. The sin in David's
life has continued to produce fruit. David journals, if I

can use that term. David is reminding himself that God is there for him. Walk with me through these verses and let's relate to David and how he viewed God as his strength.

"LORD, how are they increased that trouble me! Many are they that rise up against me." (Ps. 3:1)
David felt that as soon as trouble died down someone else rose against him. Do you feel that way sometimes? Someone takes something that you have said and makes something out of it that you didn't mean. Does it seem that there is always a negative situation going on in your life?

"Many there be which say of my soul, There is no help for him in God. Selah." (Ps. 3:2)
Sin brings consequences in the lives of God's children. We may think that there is no ending or no way out of our terrible situation, but let's read verse three.

"But thou, O LORD, art a shield for me; my glory, and the lifter up of mine head." (Ps. 3:3)
God is my shield. Ephesians 6:16 admonishes, "Above all, taking the shield of faith, wherewith ye shall be able to quench all the fiery darts of the wicked." I cannot protect myself, but I can withstand the darts that the devil throws at me if I will use the shield of faith provided by God. Picture a shield that is reflecting bullets. I am behind a Shield, safe and secure. You too are behind a Shield if you have chosen Christ. The stronger our faith base, the larger our shield will be that protects us from the "fiery darts."

I love the game of paintball. When my husband and I were in the youth ministry, paintball was one of our favorite activities. I didn't play very much; however, I enjoyed operating the video camera as the teens exited the field. They were in fighting mode, and I have some good footage from those exciting games. As the game is played, the whole point is to be able to maneuver from point to point and remain safe from your opponent. When we were saved, our "new nature" became the opponent of our "old nature." When we do not use our "shield of faith," then the "old nature" wins the battle.

God is my Glory. Nothing shines about me except that I am a child of God. I often allow my difficulties to over-shadow the glow of God's glory. When I remain behind the shield of God's protection I can stand and allow the glow of His glory to illuminate my life. The glow of His glory shines much brighter than any light that I can work up on my own.

God is my Lifter. When I allow God to be my Shield and my Glory, then He can be my Lifter. I cannot overcome the hurts of the past, present and future alone, but God comes along and takes His Hand and puts it under my chin. He lifts my chin and says, "Come on, child, it's gon-na be okay. I'm with you. You don't have to face this tri-al alone. I'm going with you through the situation. I am Your Shield, Your Glory and Your Lifter!" Just as a parent supports their child by looking in their eyes and lifting their head for encouragement, our Heavenly Father does the same for His children.

Who is God to you? Let God be your Shield, your Glory and the Lifter of your head!

Pause to Ponder

_____
_____
_____
_____
_____
_____
_____
_____
_____
_____
_____
_____
_____
_____
_____
_____
_____
_____
_____
_____
_____
_____
_____
_____

Day 6

Living By the Whatsoevers

Philippians 4:8
*"Finally, brethren, whatsoever things are true,
whatsoever things are honest, whatsoever things
are just, whatsoever things are pure, whatsoever things
are lovely, whatsoever things are of good report;
if there be any virtue, and if there be any praise,
think on these things."*

The cell phone rings. A text comes in. Social media reports something about a friend or an acquaintance, "Did you know thus and such?" What do you do? Do you talk about it feeling like it is okay because it is true? Or, do you listen but think that you won't repeat it and that will make you right before God? Information is at our fingertips every day. We take in so much, and most of the time it is information that is not good for our consumption.

Our lives take us in many directions every day. We rush here, and we participate there. We attend meetings while our thoughts are cooking dinner. We fill our calendar with people and places. Some of the schedule we love, and some of it we just endure. Celebrating birthdays, anniversaries, holidays and more, we often get caught up in the wrong thoughts concerning the people and the process.

18

What to buy, where to go, how much time to give to what event, what people think about me or what I did for them. These scenarios and more make up who we are. Philippians 4:8 challenges us with some whatsoevers.

Principle # 1
What goes in the mind will come out the mouth.

Principle # 2
You will reap what you sow and get what you grow.

Principle # 3
You cannot improve upon God's methods and words.

Principle # 4
Straddling the line of worldliness and godliness
will always be a miserable place to live.

Principle # 5
Do right. Spiritual growth only comes
when we meet God doing our part.

Let's live by the whatsoevers!

Pause to Ponder

Day 7

First Love

Revelation 2:4
"Nevertheless I have somewhat against thee, because thou hast left thy first love."

"I like you a lot," were the words I spoke to my boyfriend so many years ago. It was at a four-way stop about 2 miles from my parents home that he first said the words, "I love you" to which I replied, "I like you a lot." When we began to date, I didn't know where I was going or where I wanted to end up. He did. He had a simple plan and that was to date and marry the young lady that he had met. "I love you" were words that he said and meant with all of his heart. "I like you" were words that I meant with my heart at the time.

He immediately began to court me in such a sweet and thoughtful manner. Those first fruits of love include sweet words, acts of kindness, planning ahead, excitement when we are together and more. Once I truly loved the young man that I would marry, I began to have first love. I planned what I would wear, I waited for the phone to ring, I wrote letters every day while we were apart for college. I had first love, and the excitement and thrill of it is unforgettable.

21

After a couple is married for awhile, first love begins to wane. A couple doesn't mean for that to happen. It just happens over time because we don't always maintain what we should. Revelation 2:4 tells us that God's people strayed from their first love. First love is that intimate, exciting love for Christ that they once had. First love for Christ is demonstrated in a husband-wife relationship. First love that a husband and wife have for each other shows an outward excitement about being together. First love has actions of love and respect. First love is evident in whatever you do and wherever you go. We should not leave that first love physically, and we definitely should not leave that first love spiritually.

Think of the day you were saved. Are you still excited and thankful that God birthed you into His family? Do you still want to please Him, to be with His people, to read His Word, to show Him you love Him?

The question today is two-part: Do you have first love for your husband? Do you have first love for Christ? Ponder these thoughts today!

Pause to Ponder

_____
_____
_____
_____
_____
_____
_____
_____
_____
_____
_____
_____
_____
_____
_____
_____
_____
_____
_____
_____
_____
_____
_____
_____
_____
_____

Are You for Real?

Galatians 5:13
"For, brethren, ye have been called unto liberty;
only use not liberty for an occasion to the flesh,
but by love serve one another."

I enjoy the world of make-believe. In my childhood I pretended to be a mommy. Day after day, I played with Thumbelina and Candy, and I tried to be the best mommy that I could be for those baby dolls. My best cooking was making mud pies. The most beautiful houses were built in the branches of a tree. The "happily ever after" stories were great. My little mind loved to live in a world that didn't really exist. I was for real in my childhood, believing in the make believe!

In Matthew 15, the Pharisees are pretending to be real. They were not really for real. They put on their pretend garments and played the part of being religious. Jesus calls them pretenders in Matthew 15:7 when he says, "ye hypocrites." Their pretending was much different than my child play. Child play is just that. In child's play, the heart is genuine. The Pharisees had a bad heart. They wanted people to believe that they were spiritual when in reality their heart was carnal. Not only does Jesus call the Pharisees hypocrites or pretenders, but also he talks about why they are such. In Matthew 15:18-20, Jesus explains that the heart must be right with God if the actions and attitudes are going to produce actions and attitudes that are right with God.

Pretend means to act as though you are someone that you are not. Children can see clearly who we are. Pretending works great if you are pretending in playtime with your children; however, pretending to be spiritual does not work any better in our homes than it did for the Pharisees. Our children see us and know us. There is no fooling God or the people who know us the best, the people who live in our home.

When thinking of who you are, follow these simple thoughts:
1. Be a spiritual Christian and not a carnal one. Make your daily decisions according to God's Word and not according to what you desire to do that day.
2. Put spiritual things as top priority in your home. Family devotions and personal devotions should make your to-do list every day. The words and walk of a Christian should always be in place. Do not deceive yourself.
3. Make every day count. Have you produced any spiritual fruit today in your life? Have you planted any spiritual seeds in the life of your child today?
4. Teach and train your children with your heart and not with your head. The head produces lip service. Lip service produces rebellion because it has the root of pretense. The heart produces true and genuine fruit.
5. Examine every part of your life and ask yourself, "Am I a pretender?" After your examination, seek to make every change needed.

Are you for real?

Pause to Ponder

Day 9

My Desired Haven

Psalm 73:25
"Whom have I in heaven but thee? and there is none
upon earth that I desire beside thee."

All children have a desired age that they want to attain. Four-year-olds want to be five; Five year olds can't wait to be six. Then, they can't wait to make it to double digits, and all teens are looking for the magic from the numbers eighteen and twenty-one, and don't forget the gifts! As the years go by, my desire has changed. Although the kid in me still loves opening gifts and the traditions that our family has set for birthdays, I no longer desire to be a year older; instead, I desire quality family time!

The word *desire* can be defined as a longing for something. The word *haven* refers to a cove or shelter. In my personal quiet time with the Lord, I asked myself, "What is my desired haven concerning my life and the life of our children?" I decided to find the answer.

I found my answer in Psalm 107:21-30. These verses relate our lives to a storm. The waves of life toss us to and fro, up and down, round and round, not knowing where we will land. Verse 27 reminds us that when we are at our "wits' end," we will begin to grow spiritually. Verse 30 tells us that it is then that we will call on the Lord, our soul will receive His Word and will be quieted, and we will reach our desired haven.

The days of our lives come and go. They pass so quickly, but the wonderful truth is, as we grow older in physical years, we can grow older in spiritual years. As spiritual maturity defines us, God brings us to our desired shelter from the storms of life. We begin to take spiritual root deeper into the soil of spiritual growth.

My desire is to grow spiritually every day until I go to Heaven. My desire is for my husband and children to do the same. My desire is for my grandbabies to trust Christ at an early age and to be reared in a godly home. That is my desired haven. Really, does anything else matter? I do not have to live under the circumstances of life. No matter what takes place, I can always be at my spiritual desired haven. I love the song that says, "It's my desire to live for Jesus. It's my desire to live for Him. All through life's journey, from Earth to Glory, it's my desire to live for Him."

Ask yourself, "What is my desired haven?"

Pause to Ponder

_____
_____
_____
_____
_____
_____
_____
_____
_____
_____
_____
_____
_____
_____
_____
_____
_____
_____
_____
_____
_____
_____
_____
_____
_____

The Step of Courage

Psalm 31:24
"Be of good courage, and he shall strengthen
your heart, all ye that hope in the LORD."

I enjoy watching a baby as they take their first step. They've worked at it by letting go and standing alone for a few seconds at the time. They've tried and fallen over and over. Finally, the moment has arrived. They actually take a step! Then, they fall, but they exercised courage and took the step; so up they go, trying it again, until finally, they get it and walk.

Courage is defined as the ability to do something even though it is frightening. We are often frightened with the first step. In our Christian walk, the step of courage is very similar to the first step of a child. We are frightened to step out with courage. We are not sure if we will fail. We are uncertain about our follow through. We are insecure about that first step. Once we've stepped out in courage though, we are so glad and thankful we did.

Courageous Step One: Search for the desire that God has put in your heart. It could be buried under things that you have taken on that have masked your true value for Christ. The verse for today reminds you to "be of good courage." Don't be fearful of finding what God has put in your heart to do.

Courageous Step Two: Tell someone that can mentor you as you take your step of courage. Telling someone helps you to not feel alone. God uses people in our lives to strengthen us. Today's verse reminds us that "he shall strengthen your heart."

Courageous Step Three: Begin your journey. The beginning of a new journey can be rocky, but God will help you if you fall in the category of "all ye that hope in the Lord."

Don't miss what God has for you. Take the step of courage today!

Pause to Ponder

_____
_____
_____
_____
_____
_____
_____
_____
_____
_____
_____
_____
_____
_____
_____
_____
_____
_____
_____
_____
_____
_____
_____

Beauty for Ashes

Psalm 30:11
"Thou hast turned for me my mourning into dancing:
thou hast put off my sackcloth, and girded me
with gladness;"

I like a good trade. In elementary school, children often trade their sandwich for a more desirable snack from a friend. A boy might trade his bike for a skate board. As adults, we take our outgrown or unwanted clothing to a consignment sale. We trade what we don't want for something we do want. The main purpose of a trade is to attain something better or more useful than you already had.

The Bible talks about trading something that we have for something better. In Isaiah 61:3, the Bible tells us, "To appoint unto them that mourn in Zion, to give unto them beauty for ashes, the oil of joy for mourning, the garment of praise for the spirit of heaviness; that they might be called trees of righteousness, the planting of the LORD, that he might be glorified."

God delights in trading our ashes for beauty, our mourning for joy, our heavy heart for a spirit of praise, in order that He might be glorified. God knows your value because He created you and He longs for you to bring Him glory.

1. Trade your irresponsibility for responsibility.
2. Trade your unwilling spirit for a spirit of willingness.
3. Trade your untrustworthiness for being trustworthy.
4. Trade your stubbornness for submission to God.
5. Trade comparing yourself with others to living for others.

Make a good trade for God's glory today!

Pause to Ponder

_____
_____
_____
_____
_____
_____
_____
_____
_____
_____
_____
_____
_____
_____
_____
_____
_____
_____
_____
_____
_____
_____
_____

Day 12

Who Trained the Child?

Proverbs 10:1
*"A wise son maketh a glad father: but a foolish son
is the heaviness of his mother."*

I love being a mom. It was a joy when our three children were in the home, and it continues to be a joy as they are grown and married. As a part of the empty nest syndrome, I watched the videos of our family we have made over the years. These videos bring smiles, laughs, and tears. We had these videos transferred to DVDS and gave our children portions of their lives on DVD. How wonderful it is to go back in time and see our children when they were younger! I love hearing them express themselves in those younger days and then comparing those expressions to who they are today. It's amazing how much the same they are, but in a grown-up way.

As I view the DVDS, I can't help but ask myself, "What were they doing?" Were they obedient? Were they acting in a way that was pleasing to the Lord? Were they respectfully responding to authority?

Then, the next question I have asked myself is, "Who trained the child?" Of course, I had to ask it to myself,

36

knowing that I was their mom and was responsible for the mom part of their training. I was a stay-at-home mom for all of their younger years. It was me who disciplined every day while Dad went to work. It was me who fixed their meals and required obedience during the day. It was me who put them to nap in the morning and afternoon. It was me who trained our children to have their personal devotions every day. It was me who taught our children to honor their dad and get excited when he came home from work.

Proverbs 20:11 states, "Even a child is known by his doings, whether his work be pure, and whether it be right." The mold of a child's life begins at a very early age. A child is known for their expressions, excitement, and example. Often children mimic their parents. They talk like their parents in word and accent. They act like their parents in actions and attitudes.

As moms, it is our responsibility to lay a proper foundation for our children. Ask yourself some questions:

1. Am I a praying mom? Do I sincerely pray for my child every day?
2. Am I teaching my child to make good decisions? Do they know right from wrong?
3. Am I reaching the heart of my child? Do I touch their heart every day?
4. Do I use expressions that they can appropriately repeat?
5. Do I show excitement when my child tells me a story, does a good job, or makes a good grade?
6. Am I a good, godly example to my child? Can they mimic my actions and attitudes?
7. What do I need to change to be a better mom?
8. Am I willing to make the changes now?
9. Am I willing to change things even after my children are grown so that I will be a better mom to them and their

children?

10. Am I a mom that is growing spiritually every day?

Who is training the child? You are. Make the right changes today so that your child will grow up to be the adult that God would have them to be!

Pause to Ponder

_____
_____
_____
_____
_____
_____
_____
_____
_____
_____
_____
_____
_____
_____
_____
_____
_____
_____
_____
_____
_____
_____
_____

Day 13

The Secret Revealed

1 Corinthians 11:3
"But I would have you know, that the head of every man is Christ; and the head of the woman is the man; and the head of Christ is God."

On Friday evening, July 27, 1979, at 7:30 PM CST, I married my best friend. At 17 years of age the pews were packed, the weather was hot, I walked the aisle, we said "I do," and we have lived "happily ever after" as the saying goes. How have we survived 39 years of marriage? It's not that either of us is perfect. It's not that we never have a disagreement. What's the secret? It's the weave!

Have you ever seen someone weave a basket? When we were in Hawaii, we watched a local man weave a basket out of leaves. It was the most amazing thing. He took tree leaves and weaved the most beautiful basket. Tourists paid good money for a basket made out of free green leaves.

When a weave is done correctly, it holds together the item which it has become. It doesn't have to have extra thread or support. A successful weave is tight, secure and beautiful! Just like the weave of a basket, our marriage should be woven tightly, securely, and beautifully!

In the book of I Peter, we are told how to weave our marriage. I Peter 3:1-2 reminds us to "be in subjection to our own husbands" while they "behold our chaste conversation." Ephesians 5:22 reminds us wives to "submit yourselves unto your own husbands, as unto the Lord" and verse 23 instructs us that the "husband is the head of the wife, even as Christ is the head of the church."

God has ordained your husband to be the leader of your home; however, he cannot be if you do not allow him to be. To submit simply means to "rank under." Marriage is like a project. If no one is in charge of the project, then the project will not go forward. Your marriage cannot and will not be what it is meant to be without the leadership of the one whom God chose to be in the leadership role.

Ephesians 5:31 sums up the matter, "For this cause shall a man leave his father and mother, and shall be joined unto his wife, and they two shall be one flesh." This is a classic verse for husbands and wives. The leave, cleave and weave of marriage is summed up here. If you are going to have the marriage that God would have for you, you must first leave your parents and begin a life together. Then, you must cleave to one another. That simply means to do things together, depend on each other more than you depend on others, and keep working at it. Third, you must become one flesh. This is the weave of your marriage. Your weave will only be as tight, secure and beautiful as you make it.

When I think of one flesh I think of learning to think alike, act alike, know what the other would do or how they would respond. I think of sharing your home, your finances, your bed, your children, your life. Ephesians 5:32 refers to this as a "great mystery," comparing marriage to Christ and the church. A good and godly marriage is quite a mystery as it takes a lot of work, especially considering that often opposites attract. No matter if you married your opposite or someone just like yourself, we are all commanded to respect our husbands, and all husbands are commanded to love their wives (Ephesians 5:33). Love and respect are the key ingredients to be in place for the weave to begin. I would like to suggest 6 ways for strengthening the weave of your marriage:

1. Become close friends. A married couple should work at being true companions. Share your inner emotions and dreams with each other. Share a straw, an ice cream cone or a lollipop. Laugh together. Cry together. Do not belittle or criticize each other. The right conditions must be established in your relationship in order to share your innermost emotions. Often we build this close relationship with a friend, but not with our mate. Make a conscious effort toward this close friend relationship. Eat meals together, shop together, plan together, and play together. Allow yourself to become wholly involved in your relationship. You are either growing apart or growing closer. Have the same friends. Share the same bank account. Do not make large purchases without agreeing upon them. Spend leisure time together. Read the Bible and pray together every day. (Ecc. 4:9-12)

2. Relax together. Relaxing together brings comfort, and comfort breeds closeness. The more we relax, the more we share; and the more we share, the more we relax. Work at being comfortable in the car together. Sharing time, activities, interests, and experiences leads to shared feelings.

3. Work on oneness. Psalm 33:1 applies to the husband-wife relationship just like it does to any other, "Behold, how good and how pleasant it is for brethren to dwell together in unity." Do not fragment your relationship by going in too many directions. Do not have a closer friend than your husband. Do not keep secrets. Working

together we strengthen oneness; working apart we weaken oneness. We desire for our marriage to be strong, but we usually put emphasis on the weaknesses. A harmonious oneness should cause you to become more lovable and free to love in return.

4. Love each other. Love is a deliberate act of giving one's self to another so that the other person constantly receives enjoyment. When our love is reciprocated, then we don't just like to be together, we love to be together.

5. Like each other. You can love someone without liking them. In a moment of frustration, I have said, "I love you, but I sure don't like you right now." If you are going to like your mate, your focus should be on liking him. Dwell on what you like about him, not on what you wish he would change. Just work at liking the company of each other and liking to converse with each other. Liking your mate will strengthen your love for him.

Do you share the secret of the weave in your in your marriage?

Pause to Ponder

_____
_____
_____
_____
_____
_____
_____
_____
_____
_____
_____
_____
_____
_____
_____
_____
_____
_____
_____
_____
_____

How Is Your Health?

Proverbs 16:24
"Pleasant words are as an honeycomb, sweet to the soul,
and health to the bones."

Have you ever laughed so hard that you couldn't stop?
I remember a few occasions when I laughed uncontrol-
lably. Of course, usually you have to be there for it to
be funny. One such incident happened when our family
went to a restaurant for a meal. It was a medium fast food
place, I like to call it. The time was around 8:40 PM. The
restaurant would close in 20 minutes, and we knew that.
The employees were already sweeping and cleaning. Our
family, being 8 adults, is a bit overwhelming to such places, especially at nearly closing hours. I will never forget
the sight of the young girl sweeping the floor. When she
looked up and saw the large crowd walk in the door she
literally dropped her broom. Her mouth dropped open in
disbelief. There we stood, starving and being waited on
by this girl who obviously didn't want us there. I began to
laugh, and for months every time I thought of this occasion I would laugh so hard that I would cry. I will never
forget it. Laughter – it's good for us!

You've heard it said that laughter is the best medicine.

There may be more truth in this statement than you think, according to my research. Your sense of humor is an invaluable tool that helps you cope with a variety of daily stresses. It is said that the therapeutic advantages of laughter extend beyond its psychological benefits. In fact, some research suggests that laughter is great for your entire body.

Deep, heartfelt laughter is believed to reduce the production of stress hormones, boost the immune system, clear the respiratory tract, lower blood pressure, provide an aerobic workout for many muscles throughout the body and prevent some life-threatening diseases and heart attacks. Wow! What a list!

As Christians, we should be characterized as joyful, happy people who enjoy living. Instead we often complain about our problems as if no other person has it as bad as we do; thus, causing more physical problems rather than enjoying the life that God has given to us.

III John 2 reminds us that physical health and spiritual health are important."Beloved, I wish above all things that thou mayest prosper and be in health, even as thy soul prospereth." God doesn't give all people the same level of physical health, but it is our responsibility to care for the body that He has given to us the very best that we can. Ask yourself, "Could I be doing a better job at taking care of the body God gave to me?" If the answer is yes, do something about it.

III John then goes on to talk about our spiritual health. Spiritual health is so important to the true happiness of a person. When we are right with God, then all other relationships can be right. When we are not right with God, then we are going to have relational problems with our fellow friends and acquaintances. It is best said that when we are right vertically, then we can be right horizontally.

III John verse 3 challenges us to "walk in truth." Verse 4 is one of my most favorite verses. Even though it is not written to speak of our children born to us, that's how I like to use it. "I have no greater joy than to hear that my children walk in truth." Verse 5 speaks to us about being faithful in whatever we do, whether helping a Christian sister or brother or someone that we do not know. Verse 6 speaks of the love that we show the people with whom we rub shoulders. Verse 7 speaks of why and how we do what we do. We should do it all for God and with what God has given to us.

The verses go on to talk about some people who will not accept us. It is our responsibility to be right with God and be right with people. We are not responsible for others; only for ourselves. We cannot make people be right with us. Isn't it interesting that we can see others faults and we desire to change them, when instead we only are responsible for ourselves.

1. Laugh often.
2. Live every day to the fullest.
3. Love God supremely.
4. Learn the truth and practice what you have learned.

Physically I desire to be as healthy as I can be so that I can live a long, happy life.

Spiritually I desire to be as healthy as I can be so that I can live a victorious, Christian life!

Look for new ways to laugh, live, love and learn! How is your health?

Pause to Ponder

_____

_____

_____

_____

_____

_____

_____

_____

_____

_____

_____

_____

_____

_____

_____

_____

_____

_____

_____

_____

_____

_____

_____

Day 15

A Basket Thought

Psalm 61:2
"From the end of the earth will I cry unto thee,
when my heart is overwhelmed: lead me to the rock
that is higher than I."

Take a journey with me in to your mind's eye. Picture your mental capacity and the load that you are able to carry as a certain size of basket. God designed each of us with different styles and sizes of baskets. We all have either a small, medium, large or extra-large basket. Every day we fill our basket according to our choosing. We stretch our basket to the limit, or we don't use it to capacity. Day after day we continue to shape our basket. We allow it to stretch with a healthy usefulness, or we allow it to become hard and unchanging, all the while shrinking and becoming unhealthy and not as useful as God intended.

Frustration and busyness are often the result of a basket that is small and not so useful! We try harder, read helps books, write a schedule, but the more we plan and the harder we try, the further behind we get. When this scenario describes me, my family has heard me say many times, "My basket is overflowing."

I regularly think of this terminology, trying to consider if what I am putting in to my basket is what God would have me to fill it with. Women are expected to juggle children, home and work responsibilities while maintaing a bit of a social life. We aim to please our man, desire to appear organized to our friends and excited about the ministries that we oversee in our church. All the while, we are really just trying to hold steady, knowing that our basket is filled to capacity, and has begun to overflow.

God will never give us more than we can handle. Matthew 25:15 says, "And unto one he gave five talents, to another two, and to another one; to every man according to his several ability; and straightway took his journey." God gives us opportunities according to our abilities. We must take those opportunities and use them for God's glory. As we fill our basket with His opportunities, God will give us more opportunities. He will help us to expand our basket so that we can do more for Him.

Remember a few things:
1.   You live to glorify God.
2.   You have abilities so that you can use them for God.
3.   God gives you opportunities so that you can use your abilities for Him.
4.   God will never ask you to do anything that He knows you can't handle.
5.   As you fill your basket with the right things then God will bless and your basket will stretch according to our "several ability."
6.   Your load is not going to be the same as your friend's load, or vice versa.
7.   You can carry more than you think when you carry the load God intended for you.

Read Matthew 25:13-29 and then do a self examination. What are my "several abilities"? What is in my basket? Could I take out some things that are not necessary and put in some opportunities that God has presented to me? What size basket do I have? How can I use my "several abilities" for God's glory? Daily consider a basket thought.

Pause to Ponder

Day 16

Naughty but Cute

Proverbs 29:15
"The rod and reproof give wisdom: but a child left to himself bringeth his mother to shame."

I went with a mission's team from our church on a trip to Moldova, a small country in Eastern Europe. As we flew on this long flight, there was a 3-to 4-year-old that was sitting with his parents directly behind my husband and me. I love children, and I understand that children are not always going to do well in close settings that require restraint and quiet conditions. However, the child, who was wearing a shirt that read, "Naughty but cute" wasn't cute at all. Such a flight should lend itself to a bit of rest, think time and sleep. Not on this flight. Why? Because parents allowed behavior that should not be tolerated.

"Train up a child…" (Prov. 22:6)
Where is the training? Are parents really training their children? Are you training your children or are you giving in to your child in such a way that they inconvenience others? Proverbs 22:6 admonishes,"Train up a child in the way he should go: and when he is old, he will not depart from it."

"Even a child is known by his doings…" (Prov. 20:11)
What is your child known for? Does he/she talk respectfully, even in the beginning stages of speaking? Does your child share his/her toys? Do you correct your child for their wrong doings or do you make excuses for them? Proverbs 20:11 explains, "Even a child is known by his doings, whether his work be pure, and whether it be right."

"She saw that he was a goodly child…" (Ex. 2:2)
What is the potential of your child if you do your job correctly? Do you see who your child can become in Christ? Do you realize that you are molding your child into who they will be as an adult? Are you doing the best job that you can do? Each child is precious in the sight of God. It's up to you and me to train them to be a goodly child, respectful, loving and kind. Exodus 2:2 tells, "And the woman conceived, and bare a son: and when she saw him that he was a goodly child, she hid him three months."

"She vowed a vow…" (I Sam. 1:11)
Have you given your child to the Lord? Are you teaching and training your child according to what you ask the Lord to do with your child? Such a prayer has strings attached. "Lord, if you will do this, then I will do this." God always does His part. Are you doing yours? I Samuel 1:11 reads, "And she vowed a vow, and said, O LORD of hosts, if thou wilt indeed look on the affliction of thine handmaid, and remember me, and not forget thine handmaid, but wilt give unto thine handmaid a man child, then I will give him unto the LORD all the days of his life, and there shall no razor come upon his head."

"For this child I prayed…" (I Sam. 1:27)
You might have prayed a long time for your child. You may still be praying for your child. When God blesses, don't forget that you prayed for God to bless you with a child. Give your child back to God. They are His anyway. Allow your children to do God's will. They are safe with

Him, no matter where He may call them. I Samuel 1:27 beautifully states, "For this child I prayed; and the LORD hath given me my petition which I asked of him:"

"The heart of a child..." (Prov. 22:15)
What is in the heart of your child? Are you molding their little heart so that they will be saved when they understand the gospel? Are you daily guiding your child in their spiritual walk? The natural bend of a child is to be foolish. As a parent, you must guide and direct them so that they will desire to serve Christ from their heart. Proverbs 22:15 explains, "Foolishness is bound in the heart of a child; but the rod of correction shall drive it far from him."

"Teach them diligently..." (Duet. 6:7)
If you really desire for your child to be cute, then do your job as a parent. The Bible is so clear about how to train a child. Live by the principles in Deuteronomy 6, and you will be thankful in years to come. It's work. You can't tire of parenting before your children are grown and gone from home. Do not allow the tired parent syndrome (TPS) to set in. Deuteronomy 6:6-9 exhorts, "And these words, which I command thee this day, shall be in thine heart: And thou shalt teach them diligently unto thy children, and shalt talk of them when thou sittest in thine house, and when thou walkest by the way, and when thou liest down, and when thou risest up. And thou shalt bind them for a sign upon thine hand, and they shall be as frontlets between thine eyes. And thou shalt write them upon the posts of thy house, and on thy gates."

Naughty is a good word. My husband and I used the word when correcting our children instead of using the word *bad*. "That was naughty," we would say. It's not the child, but instead the bad things they do that are naughty.

Cute is a good word. You think your children are cute, and you should. I have many memories of my kids being so cute. I call my grandkids Cute Kids because they are absolutely adorable in my eyes! But cute and naughty do not mix. The words are a paradox!

Be a diligent parent so that "Cute but NOT naughty" can be said about your children!

Pause to Ponder

_____

_____

_____

_____

_____

_____

_____

_____

_____

_____

_____

_____

_____

_____

_____

_____

_____

_____

_____

_____

_____

_____

Whom Do You See?

1 Corinthians 13:12
"For now we see through a glass, darkly; but then
face to face: now I know in part; but then shall
I know even as also I am known."

I don't know about you, but I hesitate to check out the reflection that I see of myself in every mirror. Is my hair in place? Is my makeup still on? Do I look older today than yesterday? A mirror is a reflection of my outward appearance.

A mirror is no good without light. Have you ever tried to use a mirror when you had no light? It is a frustrating task. You can strain your eyes or change positions, but nothing matters if there is no light. A mirror has a specific purpose. Mirrors can be used when getting dressed, for décor, security, or entertainment. A mirror simply reflects things or people that you wouldn't otherwise see.

Even a broken mirror has worth because it can be repurposed. A large mirror can become a small one. A decorative mirror can become a useful one. A square mirror can be cut into a round one. Mirrors can be on the wall or on the ceiling, in the car or in the house.

My purpose today is not to focus on the mirror or the function of it, but instead on the reflection that you see in the mirror. Whom do you see when you view yourself in any type of mirror? Are you pleased with how you represent God? Are you pleased at how you represent your family? Do you only see your outward self, or can you look within and see your inward self? Our outward self is just the house that our inward self lives in.

Our Bible functions like a mirror so that you can better view your inward self. God's Word is a light for you to view who you really are. Psalm 119:130 reminds us, "The entrance of thy words giveth light; it giveth understanding unto the simple."

If a mirror is going to be any good to you, you must look into it. The same is true with God's Word. You must look into His Word to see yourself as you really are. James 1:22-25 helps you to have a clear view, "But be ye doers of the word, and not hearers only, deceiving your own selves. For if any be a hearer of the word, and not a doer, he is like unto a man beholding his natural face in a glass: For he beholdeth himself, and goeth his way, and straightway forgetteth what manner of man he was. But whoso looketh into the perfect law of liberty, and continueth therein, he being not a forgetful hearer, but a doer of the work, this man shall be blessed in his deed."

A broken mirror cannot be repaired, only repurposed. Just like a broken mirror, you can be broken and possibly cannot be restored back to your original purpose. However, God loves you and He desires for you to have a purpose for Him. You must desire to reflect God and be useful in His service even if you have to be repurposed.

II Corinthians 3:18 is a beautiful reflection of inward

beauty showing outwardly. "But we all, with open face beholding as in a glass the glory of the Lord, are changed into the same image from glory to glory, even as by the Spirit of the Lord." A quote that I love is, "Inward possession produces outward expression."

Read your Bible deliberately, thoughtfully, prayerfully, and frequently. Doing so will reflect who you really are in the mirror of God's Word. It will help you to answer such questions as, "Am I who I think I am? Am I who I want to be? Am I who God wants me to be?" Are you looking at your reflection in the mirror of God's Word?

Whom do you see?

Pause to Ponder

Yes to the Little Things

Matthew 24:46
"Blessed is that servant, whom his lord
when he cometh shall find so doing."

I'm a "yes" person. I say, "Yes, I will be happy to help you" many times when I then realize that I have overcommitted. Saying "yes" is a good thing but it does have to be kept in check. Have you ever wanted to ask someone to help you with a project because you knew that they would be great at it; then, you remembered that they usually say no to anything outside of their box. Or, maybe you didn't get the idea to ask them until a few days from the due date, and you knew they would say no because they didn't have a long time to plan the project. All of these scenarios have happened to me. It is my desire to say yes to as many people and projects as possible, but at the same time not commit to what is impossible to do.

I want to always say yes to God's call. We think about that call as something that is huge. "Here am I, Lord! Send me," is the one call that we often think of, and it is an important call for sure. However, there are often little yes's along the journey of our walk with God. Many times it is saying yes to the little things of God that will prepare us for more service to Him and will keep us directed in His perfect will.

1. Say yes to inconvenience in order that someone else might be blessed or encouraged. Allowing a travelling family to spend the night in your home, providing meals and good fellowship is an important little yes. Helping to prepare meals for a family that has suffered tragedy or that have just had a baby is a wonderful yes. Inconvenience, once it is past, is a wonderful blessing and full of rewards.

2. Say yes to a backseat role even though you have the ability to lead. You can learn from others. Leadership is a wonderful thing, but it will strengthen you to rank under another person's leadership now and then.

3. Say yes to doing the unseen, the unnoticed and even the unappreciated. Never feel that you have to tell people of the small deeds you have done. Be willing to pick up a piece of trash in the church hallway, to tidy the restroom if needed, to help another sister with her duties and not expect anything in return, or to do any unnoticed task that is not your responsibility or in your job description, whether paid or volunteer.

4. Say yes to overlooking inconsiderate treatment from others. This is a tough one. The world teaches you to get even. The Christian desires to set the situation straight or to point the finger at the person who is wronging you. The spiritual Christian will use godly discernment and wisdom, knowing that later there will be spiritual rewards for how you have respected or treated another sister in Christ. Getting even or setting the record straight is carnal and will not receive the blessing of God!

5. Say yes to being a patient listener though you may have a lot to say or add to the subject. Sometimes it is

best to listen and hear the whole story. Listen more than you speak. Do not judge or sum up a situation before you have heard. A good listener is hard to find.

6. Say yes to being sweet to the man you love. Often this is difficult because it is easy and comes natural to be mean and curt to the one you love the most! Work at it. Put it high on your list of priorities.

7. Say yes to quality time with your children. Individual time is never a waste of your time. Use it wisely while it is yours to claim. Someone said to me recently, "The days are long, but the years are short." Now, think about that one!

What would the Lord have you to say yes to? Are you willing to say yes? What other areas could be added to this list that you are thinking of? Learn to say yes to the little things so that God can better use you!

Pause to Ponder

Don't Clean Out; Clean Up

Psalm 51:2
"Wash me throughly from mine iniquity, and cleanse me from my sin."

Growing up, if my mom told me once she told me many, many times, "Sharon, don't clean out; clean up!" Why did she tell me that over and again? I finally figured it out. She would send me to my room to clean up, and I would begin cleaning out a drawer or the closet. I absolutely loved to clean out, so that's exactly what I would do. Obviously, cleaning out would make more of a mess than just cleaning up, at least for the immediate time. But, if you think about it, cleaning out was best if it was done well; that way the job was done in a more thorough fashion than just making the room look presentable.

For years I have had a house of my own to clean. What is most interesting is that I find myself cleaning out when I only have the time to clean up. When it happens, I chuckle inside, realizing that the little girl that I was is still inside me! It is good for every home to be thoroughly cleaned at least once per year. The closets tend to collect all kinds of "not-sure-what-to-do-with items," and the drawers, well, they tend to gobble up odd socks and unique items of interest. The baseboards need dusting, the windows need washing, and you and I are the ones to get the job done.

As much as your house might need a thorough cleaning, I would like for you to think about your life. You don't just need to clean up your life; you need to clean out your life. Once per year is not enough for this area of cleaning. It is necessary to stay on top of cleaning your life each and every day. When debris builds up, it is natural to become spiritually slack and unable to grow as God would have you to. Jesus clearly spoke about this subject to the scribes and Pharisees in Matthew 23:25-26: "Woe unto you, scribes and Pharisees, hypocrites! for ye make clean the outside of the cup and of the platter, but within they are full of extortion and excess. Thou blind Pharisee, cleanse first that which is within the cup and platter, that the outside of them may be clean also." The religious leaders were having a problem. They were pretending to be clean, religious people when, in reality, their hearts were unclean. Jesus was not pleased. He plainly told them to clean the inside, and the outside would follow.

You would not clean your closets and drawers and leave the rooms in your house unkempt. You would however, vacuum and clean up for company to come, leaving the closets shut tight so that no one could see them. Proverbs 4:23 explains spiritual house cleaning: "Keep thy heart with all diligence; for out of it are the issues of life." Your life will be clean when your heart is clean.

So ask yourself, "What's in my heart? Is it clean? How can I keep my heart?" What needs cleaning out of my heart so that my life will be clean?

Instead of the saying, "Don't clean out; clean up," say about your life, "Don't clean up; clean out!"

Pause to Ponder

Heartwebs

Proverbs 4:23
"Keep thy heart with all diligence;
for out of it are the issues of life."

Up in the corners, near the baseboards, in light fixtures, and other places, there they are: cobwebs. I don't know how or when they get there. They just show up. Sometimes they are too high to reach, so I'm jumping with broom or duster in hand, trying to knock them down. The next thing I know there are dust bunnies that have gotten caught up in the webs. Our half bath has this problem at the bottom left corner of the sink counter. I have gotten rid of this little web over and over, but something funny always happens. It's not too long before, you guessed it, the cobweb is back again.

Why is that? Why do the cobwebs return to the very same place? The answer is actually quite simple. It is because I only got rid of the cobweb. I did not get rid of the source of the cobweb. The source of the cobweb is always an 8-legged arachnid. We call it a spider! All cobwebs are made by spiders of some type. I don't like the thought that a spider is lurking in the cracks, waiting for a time that he can come out and spin his web.

A spider spins a web to slow down or catch whatever comes its way. As I studied cobwebs, I learned that they can be destroyed with any tool, water, or lava. (I'm especially glad I learned about the lava technique.) If you want to rid your home of cobwebs, you must get rid of the spiders. In order to do that, you must treat them at the foundation of your home with insecticide. Protection is needed when you treat them because they can bite you. So, wear gloves.

The study of cobwebs is interesting and definitely reminds me of cobwebs that get in to each of our hearts. Psalm 51:10 clearly tells us, "Create in me a clean heart, O God; and renew a right spirit within me." The heart is our foundation of spiritual things. If the heart is clean, the life is clean. To state it in spider terms, the foundation must be treated to rid your heart of webs.

Let's refer to the webs of our heart as Heartwebs. These Heartwebs prevent us from experiencing victorious Christian living through Christ Jesus our Lord. Heartwebs, like cobwebs, are all formed from one source. That source is sin, and it manifests itself in different forms. Just like spiders form different types of webs, people hide different sins in their lives and think they can get by with it. The Heartwebs, like the cobwebs, begin to show. No longer is the sin hidden. It has begun to form a Heartweb. The Heartwebs manifest themselves in our attitude, personality, things we do, places we go, and people we hang around. We can't actually see the sin that is deeply hidden in our hearts, but we can see the web that it spins on the outside.

Heartwebs take on all kinds of personalities and configurations like injustice, insecurity, discouragement, disillusionment, depression, bitterness, ruptured relationships, rejection, accusations and other webs. In order to get rid of the Heartwebs, we must rid ourselves of the sin that has crept into the corners of our hearts.

1. Understand that sin is in every person's life. The spider of sin can manifest itself in many different types of Heart-webs. Proverbs 30:28 reminds us that "The spider taketh hold with her hands, and is in kings' palaces." This verse simply reminds us that spiders can go anywhere. They come into your house, my house or the king's palace in small, dark places. Likewise, sin lurches in the recesses of our hearts.

2. Consider your protection. The Devil loves it when we do not recognize sin for what it really is. He uses this tactic regularly to defeat good, Christian people just like you and me! So, put on the whole armour of God as stated in Ephesians 6:11-17.

3. Clean the foundation of your life which is your heart. Use the proper insecticides which are your Bible, prayer and the principle of replacement. The Bible has all of the answers. Individual verses will pinpoint each source. Use each verse as God intended. Ask God's forgiveness for your sin, calling the source by name. Exercise the principle of replacement. Replace old habits of the heart with new spiritual habits of the heart.

Ask yourself these questions:
Is what I am doing, thinking or feeling stealing my joy? (Ps. 51:12)
Is what I am doing, thinking or feeling giving Satan the upper hand? (II Cor. 2:9-11)
Is what I am doing, thinking or feeling quenching the Holy Spirit? (I Thess. 5:19)
Is what I am doing, thinking or feeling breaking fellowship with God? (Is. 59:1-2)

Put on protection (the whole armor of God), get your insecticide (Bible, prayer and principle of replacement) and let's kill the spiders (sin) so the Heartwebs vanish from our lives! What kinds of Heartwebs do you have?

Pause to Ponder

_____

_____

_____

_____

_____

_____

_____

_____

_____

_____

_____

_____

_____

_____

_____

_____

_____

_____

_____

_____

_____

_____

_____

_____

_____

Day 21

Stressed Out

Matthew 6:25-27
"Therefore I say unto you, Take no thought for your life,
what ye shall eat, or what ye shall drink; nor yet
for your body, what ye shall put on. Is not the life more
than meat, and the body than raiment? Behold the
fowls of the air: for they sow not, neither do they reap,
nor gather into barns; yet your heavenly Father feedeth
them. Are ye not much better than they? Which of you
by taking thought can add one cubit unto his stature?"

Have you ever used the phrase "stressed out"? Probably
so. And, you probably are. We are all stressed about many
things. Good things! Right priorities! The daily routine of
life! Just thinking about the subject causes your mind to
race from event to event, from responsibility to responsibility, and once again the subject consumes your mind,
"I'm stressed out!"

Priorities are responsibilities in our lives that we must
give attention to. My husband prioritizes his life with 5
p's, "To be the person I ought to be, to be the partner I
ought to be, to be the parent I ought to be, to be the papa I
ought to be, to be the pastor I ought to be." This is actually
a great prioritized list to live by, but even when prioritiz-

74

ing in this way there can be conflicts of priorities, duties that pile on top of each other and insufficient time to accomplish all that lies on our plates.

When we realize the conflict of priorities, stress begins to build up in our lives. The muscles tighten, the brain malfunctions, the chores mount, and we feel trapped in a spin cycle that seems impossible to overcome. There is good and bad stress in each of our lives. Bad stress comes when we worry about things that we can do absolutely nothing about. Admitting that you just might have some bad stress could help you to be an overcomer; so, come on, admit it along with me!

Luke 10:40 tells us that Martha has some bad stress going on. "But Martha was cumbered about much serving, and came to him, and said, Lord, dost thou not care that my sister hath left me to serve alone? bid her therefore that she help me." I picture Martha worrying about getting the perfect meal ready and not having any help. She had begun to stew about this. Her thoughts were running out of control. The Bible addresses this kind of unnecessary, bad stress many times including Philippians 4:6 and II Corinthians 10:5. On more than one occasion, I have been awakened in the middle of a good night's rest with a thought that I could not let go. I had allowed that situation to build into a negative thought which created bad stress. Martha placed priority on the meal instead of the Master who was attending the meal. Excellence should be sought after in the life of a Christian; however, it has its proper place.

Good stress actually comes from the busyness of good things in our lives. We really wouldn't want to change any of these things. There seems to be too many things calling our name at the same time. The priorities list for me of wife, parent, nana, and others surmounts like a huge mountain that is impossible to climb on many occasions.

I really do not see anything in my life that I want to drop. I love being a supportive wife. I love being the parent of my adult kids and involving myself in their lives. I love being nana to 7 Cute Kids with the 8th on the way. I love spending time with others in my life that are friends and acquaintances. These areas of my life have many sprouts off of them that cause good stress. Mostly the area of time to be with, do with, and be a part of everything that attaches to these areas of my life.

You have the same in your life. The good stress and the bad stress lean us toward being stressed out! The 7-day week, the 24-hour day, the weekly and daily commitments, and more. What are we going to do?

Ask yourself these questions?
1.   Am I prone to good and bad stress?
2.   Do I feel trapped in my stressed-out life?
3.   Do I give advice to others about their schedule?
4.   Do I take my own advice?
5.   Am I working toward a solution which would include proper rest, exercise and balance?

I have asked myself these questions ,and my answers are embarrassingly human. Yours probably are too; so let's make a list of thoughts and get to work.

1.   Remember that God created the 7-day week with 24 hours in a day, and God created you and me to live in this time structure.
2.   We must remind ourselves that God understands our time limitations and human abilities.
3.   Determine to live as God expects us to and not as we feel pressure from others to live.
4.   Learn to say no to worldly reasoning and negative thoughts.
5.   Understand that you can truly prioritize one person or event at a time. Multi-tasking priorities is impossible, and

we are fooling ourselves to believe differently.

6.   We are not trapped in stress unless we close the door to setting and keeping right priorities.

7.   Pray and ask God to give you wisdom and guidance.

8.   Look to God's Word for instruction.

We only have one life to live. Will we live stressed out or will we enjoy the journey?

Pause to Ponder

Day 22

It's Whom You Know that Counts

Esther 4:14
*"For if thou altogether holdest thy peace at this time,
then shall there enlargement and deliverance arise to the
Jews from another place; but thou and thy father's house
shall be destroyed: and who knoweth whether thou art
come to the kingdom for such a time as this?"*

One Monday evening I received a disturbing phone call from my sister. She began to tell me about the condition that my mom was found in that afternoon. As we spoke, my mom was being taken to the hospital by ambulance in critical condition. I felt helpless as I listened to what was happening. Many questions flooded my heart and mind. Tears filled my eyes as I wondered what the next 24 hours held. My husband and I boarded a plane to Alabama in the next few hours. We found my mom in a very lethargic state due to carbon dioxide poisoning.

Our family stayed in the CCU waiting area so that we could visit Mama every opportunity possible. As we visited her, we took note of her progress. It would go forward and backward as many of you know who have sat in the same seat with someone you love. Was it time for our mom to go to Heaven? Were the doctors doing all that they could do? Such questions flooded our hearts and minds as we tried to make the best decisions possible. Thanks to a large support of family and friends, we were not alone in comfort and prayers.

Finally, after determining that Mom was not getting the best attention needed, my niece stepped up and said, "I know someone in administration. I will meet with him." And you know the rest of the story. It's not what you know, but whom you know that counts.

Spiritually speaking, the statement rings true as well. It's not what you know, but Whom you know that counts. You know Bible verses, but ask yourself, "Do I know the Author of those verses? I know about God, but do I really know Him?"

1. Know for sure that you are saved.
I John 5:13 - "These things have I written unto you that believe on the name of the Son of God; that ye may know that ye have eternal life, and that ye may believe on the name of the Son of God."

2. Read your Bible daily so that you get to know your Creator, Savior, and Heavenly Father.
Acts 17:11 - "These were more noble than those in Thessalonica, in that they received the word with all readiness of mind, and searched the scriptures daily, whether those things were so."

3. Have regular times of prayer and perhaps use a prayer journal.
I Thessalonians 5:17 - "Pray without ceasing."

4. Choose some promises to claim from God's Word.
Philippians 4:6-7 - "Be careful for nothing; but in every

thing by prayer and supplication with thanksgiving let your requests be made known unto God. And the peace of God, which passeth all understanding, shall keep your hearts and minds through Christ Jesus."

God's peace is conditional. Don't worry about anything. Pray about everything. Be thankful in all situations, and God's peace will rule your life.

5. Chart your spiritual growth by journaling what you have learned each day from God's Word.
Psalm 139:2-4 - "Thou knowest my downsitting and mine uprising, thou understandest my thought afar off. Thou compassest my path and my lying down, and art acquainted with all my ways. For there is not a word in my tongue, but, lo, O LORD, thou knowest it altogether."

Psalm 139:23-24 - "Search me, O God, and know my heart: try me, and know my thoughts: And see if there be any wicked way in me, and lead me in the way everlasting."

For my mom, we believe that talking to someone in administration made all the difference in her care, which in turn, saved her life. The same is true with your spiritual health. I know that you will agree, "It's not what you know, but Whom you know that counts."

Pause to Ponder

Sculpting a Balanced Life

1 Thessalonians 5:23
"And the very God of peace sanctify you wholly;
and I pray God your whole spirit and soul and body
be preserved blameless unto the coming
of our Lord Jesus Christ."

I am not into art and sculpture; however, I did read about the sculpture named *David*, and it captured my attention. The sculpture stands in Florence, Italy, at the Galleria dell' Accademia. *David* is a masterpiece that was sculpted between 1501 and 1504 by the Italian artist Michelangelo. It is a marble statue that stands 17 feet in the air. It took Michelangelo 3 years to finish his work. He lived, breathed and slept this sculpture to its completion.

The illustration intrigued me so much that I googled "how to make a sculpture." This is what I found: First, you brainstorm. Exactly what kind of sculpture are you trying to make? Do you want your sculpture to have a meaning? What look do you want it to have? Second, you collect what you would like your sculpture to be made of. Some are made of candy wrappers, glass bottles, or scrap metal. Others are made of some type of clay or material that will harden. Third, you must make a base. All sculptures must have something to hold them up. The base can be showing or not showing. The most steady base is made of metal. Fourth, you must use a good paste appropriate for the materials in order for the sculpture to stay together. Some sculptures may not need paste, depending on the material you choose for your masterpiece. If paste is needed for your material, it is like bread to a sandwich. Fifth, your sculpture needs character. It needs to be personalized by its owner in order to reveal its true beauty and worth. Sixth, consider painting or not painting your sculpture. This depends on the look you are trying to achieve. It depends on what you want to stand out in your sculpture.

Sculpting a balanced life has many resemblances to forming a sculpture. Think about it. First, brainstorm. When I brainstorm about myself, what kind of sculpture do I see? What am I making of my life? Second, what am I collecting that makes my life? Am I making a collection of things that matter or things that are immaterial? Third, what is my base made of? My base should be founded on God's Word. When I stand on the Bible, then I must make decisions that lend to a sculpture He is pleased with. Fourth, what paste holds me together? The paste of faith, family and friends is the best! Fifth, what about the character that makes up your life? What are you known for? Rudeness, sharp tongue, lack of focus, inability to complete a project, moodiness and such are core character flaws that need to be altered so that we can better represent our Sculptor. Ask yourself, what characterizes my life? Sixth is the paint. Ask yourself, "What colors my life? What stands out? Does the paint need to be brightened or toned differently?"

Ask yourself these questions and consider balance or imbalance in these six areas. What can I change? How can I do it?

1. Change happens gradually even though we may make

the decision to change instantly. A baby grows slowly, and one day you realize that they are not a baby anymore.

2. Keep your emotions in check. They can work for or against you. When you keep your emotions in balance all those whom you love benefit from it.

3. Restructure thought patterns. Romans 12:2 and II Corinthians 10:5 are great verses to live by. You cannot control the things that happen to you each day or the things that come into your life, but you can control how you think about them.

4. Get a right perspective. It changes how a situation is viewed and the effects that it has on a person after the situation occurs. A negative perspective helps you see negative, and a positive perspective helps you to see the positive in everyone and everything.

5. Stay in control of your actions. It is possible to face things out of my control and not act out of control. When someone is out of control, relationships are damaged, strained, hurt and more difficulties face us, causing more stress and struggles.

6. Fix your mind on God. The display of temper, selfishness, negativity and warped perspective proves whether our mind is fixed on God or ourselves.

7. See beyond what is and view what could be. Who could you become "in Christ"? II Corinthians 5:17 shows a picture of a beautiful, spiritual sculpture. What can God do with your life if you turn everything over to Him?

8. Stop labeling yourself. Condemning statements such as "I always mess things up" or "I am so stupid" help no one and get nothing accomplished.

9. Admit your issues of imbalance and do something about them. Such issues as busyness, out-of-control children, keeping a clean house, quality family time, organization, self-esteem, and relationship issues must be balanced in order to live a productive, Christian life, pleasing to God.

10. Begin chiseling away what is not balanced in your life. Imbalance has no proper place of importance and is never productive.

Let's go back to the *David* sculpture. Michelangelo was the completer of the sculpture but not the originator. Initially, the 17-foot block of marble was the project of an artist named Agostino di Duccio. After shaping some of the legs, feet and torso, he inexplicably abandoned the work. Ten years later, an artist named Antonio Rossellino was hired to complete it, but his contract was cancelled. It was 25 years before Michelangelo, just 26 years old then, picked up a chisel and dared to believe he could complete this masterpiece. Sources say that Michelangelo never left his *David*. For more than two years he worked on and slept beside the 6-ton slab of marble whose subject called to him from inside the unchiseled places. When at last the 17-foot David emerged, Michelangelo is reported to have said, "I saw the angel in the marble and carved until I set him free." When asked how he made his statue, Michelangelo is reported to have said, "It is easy. You just chip away the stone that doesn't look like David."

God doesn't allow imbalance in your life to keep you captive, or so that you will label yourself, but instead to allow Him to chisel away until you are molded as He chooses. Ask yourself: does balance need to be sculpted in my life?

Pause to Ponder

_____
_____
_____
_____
_____
_____
_____
_____
_____
_____
_____
_____
_____
_____
_____
_____
_____
_____
_____
_____
_____
_____
_____
_____
_____

What Makes a Mother?

II Timothy 1:5
"When I call to remembrance the unfeigned faith
that is in thee, which dwelt first in thy
grandmother Lois, and thy mother Eunice;
and I am persuaded that in thee also."

Favorites. What are favorite things? Something that I favor is something that I prefer more than something else. I do have some favorite things in my life. I'm sure you do too if you stop and think about it. Think with me as I mention a few. I have a favorite place to get on my knees and pray in our house. My favorite way to sleep is to sleep through a rain storm as the constant sound of the rain pecks on the roof. My favorite breakfast foods are oatmeal or grits with plenty of butter. My favorite meal is a huge salad with a chicken breast on top. My favorite ice cream is vanilla with white chocolate chips and M&M's mixed in.

I have a favorite oldest child, a favorite middle child and a favorite youngest child. They know that they are my "favorite" in their own special way. I would say that I have a favorite husband but something just doesn't sound right about that, so I'll say that some of my favorite time spent is with my husband! My favorite color is navy blue. My favorite vacation is anywhere that our family is together and enjoying each other's company. These are only a few of my favorite things.

I also have some favorite Bible verses. These verses challenge me to live for the Lord, to stay focused on His plan for my life and to continue to grow spiritually in my daily walk with Him. As I share some of these verses with you, think with me how these verses apply to your personal life.

My life verse is Philippians 4:19 - "But my God shall supply all your need according to his riches in glory by Christ Jesus." I love to dwell on the truth that God provides for my every need.

One of my favorite passages on child rearing is Deuteronomy 6:3-9. Child rearing is 24/7. Don't miss out on training your "favorites."

The verse that has helped me to grow spiritually is I John 5:13 – "These things have I written unto you that believe on the name of the Son of God; that ye may know that ye have eternal life, and that ye may believe on the name of the Son of God." This verse was life-changing for me when I realized that I could know for sure that I was saved. I was eighteen years old when I discovered that truth. Once I knew how to live beyond doubt, then I could grow spiritually day-by-day in my Christian walk with the Lord.

When I share the plan of salvation with someone, I have two verses that are my favorite. In Romans 6:23, I love to emphasize the word *but* because the two parts of the verse are such a contrast. "For the wages of sin is death; but the gift of God is eternal life through Jesus Christ our Lord." The second verse that is so special to me is Romans

10:13 – "For whosoever shall call upon the name of the Lord shall be saved." I love to tell a person that *whosoever* is the most beautiful word in the Bible because it includes me and it includes you. Many times, a tear trickles down a hurting lady's cheek when she realizes that she too is a "whosoever" to the God who created all things.

My favorite story in the Bible is the story of Ruth and her daughters-in-law. My heart is stirred each time I read of the choices that each daughter-in-law made. I have two daughters-in-law, and I'm so thankful for their decision to follow their husbands as he follows Christ.

The Bible character that challenges my heart over and again is Solomon. In Ecclesiastes 2, I am challenged to learn what was vanity in Solomon's life and to apply what Solomon learned so that I don't have to say the same about any part of my life. Ecclesiastes 2:11 reveals his epiphany: "Then I looked on all the works that my hands had wrought, and on the labor that I had labored to do: and, behold, all was vanity and vexation of spirit, and there was no profit under the sun."

These are only a few of my favorite things. What are some of yours? Count your favorites and list your verses. It will be good for you to name a few of your favorite things!

Pause to Ponder

Day 25

Spiritual Habits of the Heart

Proverbs 23:19
"Hear thou, my son, and be wise,
and guide thine heart in the way."

Habits are hard to break whether they are good or bad habits. All of us are habitual people. For example, think about where you sit in church. If you are like me, you sit in the same spot every service. What about habits that you have developed in your home? I take off my jewelry and put it in the same place each day. I fold towels the same way. I keep my pots and pans in the same cabinet, and I put my purse on the same counter.

When we think about it, we are definitely people of habit. The habits that I have referred to are not good or bad; they are just habits. Habits such as these could be good, better, or best, according to the organization of our home; however, here are some habits that are good or bad. Let's refer to these habits as spiritual habits of the heart.

Spiritual habits of the heart include daily Bible study and prayer. They include our attitude, thoughts, actions and reactions as all of these areas affect who we really are and who we are becoming in our day-to-day lives.

When I think of spiritual habits of the heart, the first people that come to mind are Lot and his wife. Luke 17:32 tells us to "Remember Lot's wife." Why does this passage include these three words? We read about the story of Lot and his wife in Genesis 12-14. What a sad story as we read of the choices that Lot made for his wife. When Lot separated from his Uncle Abraham, he could have still made good, spiritual choices, but he didn't. He chose to pitch his tent toward Sodom (13:12). This choice shows us that Lot had begun to slack in the area of spiritual habits of the heart. He had begun to form habits of the heart that were going to lead him and his family down a road of hurt and heartache.

Genesis 19:26 is a very sad verse: "But his wife looked back from behind him, and she became a pillar of salt." Lot's wife left her heart in Sodom. As she was being rushed out of the city, she thought of the lifestyle she was leaving behind. She was not able to tell her friends good-bye. She was not given enough time to gather her material possessions. So, in the rush of it all, she did what her heart practiced on a daily basis. Lot's wife looked back at what she loved, the worldly ways of Sodom. Because it was her habit, she naturally leaned that way even though God had given her one last chance to escape and live.

It is important to practice the right spiritual habits of the heart. Somehow we believe that God is going to come down and put some spell on us that makes us desire to read our Bible for 1 hour per day without struggle. This spell is going to put a desire in our heart to never miss church or never say a bad word or never do a bad deed. This is a wrong philosophy. God does not do for us what we can do for ourselves. I love this quote by Oswald Chambers when he refers to II Peter 1:5, "And beside this, giving all diligence, add to your faith virtue; and to virtue knowledge." "We are in danger of forgetting that we cannot do what God does, and that God will not do what we can do. We cannot save ourselves nor sanctify ourselves, God does that; but, God will not give us good habits, He will not give us character, He will not make us walk aright. We have to do all that ourselves. We have to work out the salvation God has worked in. 'Add' means to get into the habit of doing things."

The right philosophy is, "I know it is right to read my Bible daily, so I will do it." Because I read my Bible, God gives me understanding. By doing the right thing, I develop a deep desire to learn more and read more from God's Word! "I know that it is right to be faithful to church, so I will do it." Because I go to church, the Lord blesses me more than if I stayed home and selfishly had my way.

Examine the spiritual habits of your heart. Would your habit have been to look back, yearning for the worldly ways of Sodom? Or would your habit have been to follow the leading of the Holy Spirit, fearing God, and knowing that you must do exactly as He asked you to do without any hesitation or doubt?

What are your spiritual habits of the heart?

Pause to Ponder

_____
_____
_____
_____
_____
_____
_____
_____
_____
_____
_____
_____
_____
_____
_____
_____
_____
_____
_____
_____
_____
_____

Fulfilling Love

Hebrews 13:1
"Let brotherly love continue."

Brotherly love is a favorite subject of mine. One of my favorite pictures is my Daddy with his two brothers. They are sitting on the front porch of the house they were raised in. A friend and I were visiting in Alabama when we walked up on these three brothers sitting on the porch, just taking a break. I said, "Freeze just like you are." The picture depicts true brotherly love. These brothers love each other, work together on projects and eat lunch together every Saturday. I call this kind of love and care, "Fulfilling Love!" I love these men, and I get teary-eyed speaking of their love and care for each other.

I have tried to instill this kind of love in our own children. No one understands you, goes to bat for you and can truly support you like your own brother or sister; that is, if siblings make the choice to love and support each other in a loving, biblical manner. It was our goal as our children were young to begin this process. We used several areas of training such as doing work projects together, playing together, having weekly family fun, making a big deal about family birthday parties and with all of these things promoting sibling friendship. It is my desire for our three children, three in-laws, and grandchildren to understand "Fulfilling Love!"

The Bible speaks of brotherly love.

Romans 12:10 - "Be kindly affectioned one to another with brotherly love; in honour preferring one another;" Have a soft spot in your heart towards your brother; to support them and not talk negatively about them.

I Thessalonians 4:9 - "But as touching brotherly love ye need not that I write unto you: for ye yourselves are taught of God to love one another." Paul deems it necessary to bring up the subject of brotherly love, but he feels no need to harp on it because we know what the Bible tells us about it.

Hebrews 13:1 - "Let brotherly love continue." Our love for our blood brothers and sisters as well as our Christian brothers and sisters should be a continuous love, and a continuous love without criticism and hypocrisy is "Fulfilling Love."

Of course, these brotherly love verses include our blood siblings but are not exclusive to such. They extend to our brothers and sisters in Christ. If you have a good relationship with your blood brothers and sisters, then apply the principles of support to your brothers and sisters in Christ. Knowing that you shouldn't gossip about your blood sister, then don't gossip about your Christian sister. As you plan time to spend with your blood sister to build your relationship, then understand the importance and plan to spend time with your Christian sister to build your relationship with her.

Work faithfully at fulfilling love!

Pause to Ponder

_____

_____

_____

_____

_____

_____

_____

_____

_____

_____

_____

_____

_____

_____

_____

_____

_____

_____

_____

_____

_____

_____

Peace of Mind

Psalm 29:11
*"The LORD will give strength unto his people; the
LORD will bless his people with peace."*

Do you need peace of mind today? Do you live under your circumstances? Do you feel like you need to come apart before you come apart?

Several years ago, my husband and I went on a get-away trip to a small cabin in Pigeon Forge, Tennessee. The cabin set off the main road, down two or three small roads and up a washed path to a trail with a sign that said "Southern Nites." At this secluded place we spent four nights. If I think about it, it was actually kind of scary – you know, being so by yourself and all alone. I guess we didn't feel too frightened though because when we went out about 1:00 the next afternoon, we actually found the key still in the door from entering the night before.

What a reminder of the peace of God in the following verses:

Psalm 46:10 - "Be still and know that I am God."

Philippians 4:7 - "And the peace of God, which passeth all understanding, shall keep your hearts and minds through Christ Jesus."

Colossians 3:15 - "And let the peace of God rule in your hearts, to the which also ye are called in one body; and be ye thankful."

1. Pray for peace of mind. The Bible says in Jeremiah 33:3,"Call unto me, and I will answer thee, and shew thee great and mighty things, which thou knowest not."

2. Prioritize your priorities. Many things must be done, but there are some that are much more important than others.

3. Put your best foot forward. There is never regret when you do a job well.

4. Plan your daily schedule with Jesus in mind. Ask yourself, "Is the Lord Jesus pleased with my daily schedule?"

5. Pray again. Peace of mind only comes from our Heavenly Father. Prayer must be on going. We must have a prayer life, not a prayer time.

6. Participate in activities that give you peace of mind. Go with your family on an outing. Read your favorite book. Go to a serene place to think, maybe on your deck or to the park. Write down your thoughts.

7. Proceed in an upward direction. We must go forward because it is right, not because we feel like it.

When I am in the quietness of the surroundings of a cabin, peace of mind is so readily available. It is also available to me in the busyness of the city because peace of mind comes to me through the power of the Holy Spirit who dwells within my body.

Ask yourself, "Do I have peace of mind?" If not, it is available for you today!

Pause to Ponder

The Mystery of Wisdom

Proverbs 2:6
"For the LORD giveth wisdom: out of his mouth
cometh knowledge and understanding."

Do you like mysteries? Some people love to solve mysteries. There are board games that are mysteries. You can read mystery books. Some television shows are about mysteries. Writers and producers love to keep their audience in suspense with mysteries.

Personally, I don't like mysteries. I like to play board games that are easy to play, fun for all, and not such brain work. I like to read books that are helpful, and I like a simple plot in a television show that I can keep up with as I check email, fold clothes, or do other household tasks.

I Corinthians 2:7 speaks of the mystery of the wisdom of God. "But we speak of the wisdom of God in a mystery, even the hidden wisdom which God ordained before the world unto our glory." God's wisdom is a mystery that was hidden, and then it was revealed through Christ and the Holy Spirit helps each one of God's children to understand the wisdom of God and how to apply it to their lives. The Corinthian people had the wisdom of God available to them; however, they didn't apply it. They did not listen to the Holy Spirit. They chose to live by the knowledge of men. They were carnal Christians. (I Cor. 3:1)

Understanding the wisdom of God lies in our willingness to give full leading of our lives to the Holy Spirit. We, as individuals, cannot know God or His wisdom apart from the Holy Spirit. The Holy Spirit knows the wisdom of God because the Holy Spirit is God. The Holy Spirit is the link between God and man, thus giving us opportunity to know the wisdom of God and to follow His leading in our lives.

The wisdom of God for each of our lives is a mystery that remains unsolved for many Christians. We fail to solve the mystery of His wisdom for our daily lives, when it is really quite simple. Wisdom awaits us as we yield to the Holy Spirit's leading in our lives.

I decided to google how to solve a mystery, and this is what I found:

1.   Use a magnifying glass to search the perimeter of the crime scene. Find if anything is missing. Search for fingerprints or traces of the enemy.
2.   Use a notebook and pencil to write down any evidence and data that the crime scene has. Write down anything that you see may lead you to any witnesses or suspects that may have something, or absolutely nothing, to do with the mystery.
3.   Take in your suspects and put them into questioning. Ask the questions that may need to be asked due to the evidence from your notebook. Put them on a lie detector test.
4.   Investigate the area and look for fingerprints. If any match the suspect's fingerprints, then take that suspect, or the suspects, in for questioning one more time.
5.   Come to a conclusion of the case. If you have the

wrong guy, examine the area again. The probability of getting the wrong guy is less than the probability of the case happening in the first place.

The same 5 principles can be put to work with spiritual application.
1.   Use the magnifying glass of God's Word to search the perimeters of your heart. Do you find traces of the world in your daily life? Do you find man's knowledge or God's wisdom?
2.   Use a notebook and pen to journal what you have read in God's Word. Writing down what it means to you at the time will help you to apply what you know is needed in order to daily live with God's wisdom.
3.   Question the things in your life that are influencing you. Are your friends influencing you to live right? Are the places you go causing you to think wrong thoughts or participate in wrong activities? Can you be a witness where you are and what you are doing? Are you lying to yourself at possessing God's wisdom for your life?
4.   Look for evidences in your life that will incriminate you as a growing Christian. Make a list of those evidences. If there are no evidences, immediately make changes in your life.
5.   Come to a conclusion concerning the mystery of wisdom in your own life. Do you have God's wisdom for your life? Are you seeking after God's wisdom by submitting to the leading of the Holy Spirit in your life?

"If any of you lack wisdom, let him ask of God, that giveth to all men liberally, and upbraideth not; and it shall be given him." (James 1:5) The mystery of wisdom is simple: ask for it and apply it!

Pause to Ponder

Day 29

Truths from Toddlers

Mark 10:14
*"But when Jesus saw it, he was much displeased,
and said unto them, Suffer the little children
to come unto me, and forbid them not: for of such
is the kingdom of God."*

Jesus uses the term "little ones" 6 times in the New Testament. Every one of us would agree that Jesus loves all of the children of the world. These little ones are precious to Jesus, and they are precious to us. Toddlers are young, innocent, sweet, loving and teachable; yet they are teachers. So many lessons can be learned from these little ones.

I often tell our grandbabies to lay on their stomach and I do "X marks the spot with a dot, dot, dot…" on their back. They lay so still while I draw on their backs. Then, it's their turn, and they try to do the same to me. Hide and Seek is so much fun. The kids hide before naptime, and I find them. Of course, they choose the same spots over and over. They get extremely excited when I begin to count, call their name and search for them. I enjoy every minute of these bonding times. They listen and learn so quickly. It's more than fun. It is time for me to teach and them to learn and a time for me to learn and them to teach!

1. *Toddlers love unconditionally.* A toddler loves all who spend time with them. Their kisses are waiting, their words are freely given, and their hugs are tight and often. Matthew 22:37, 39 - "Jesus said unto him, Thou shalt love the Lord thy God with all thy heart, and with all thy soul, and with all thy mind. And the second is like unto it, Thou shalt love thy neighbour as thyself."
Ask yourself, "Do I love unconditionally?"

2. *Toddlers forgive immediately.* If you have ever accidentally stepped on a toddler's toe or knocked over their toy, then you realize their forgiving spirit. As soon as you offer your apology, they are ready and willing to accept it with no strings attached. They are even forgiving to each other.
Matthew 18:21, 35 - "Then came Peter to him, and said, Lord, how oft shall my brother sin against me, and I forgive him? till seven times? So likewise shall my heavenly Father do also unto you, if ye from your hearts forgive not every one his brother their trespasses."
Ask yourself, "Do I forgive immediately?"

3. *Toddlers laugh easily.* Have you ever turned over the tickle bucket of a toddler? It is precious.
Psalm 5:11 - "...let them also that love thy name be joyful in thee."
Ask yourself, "Do I laugh easily? Am I a joyful Christian?"

4. *Toddlers share, sometimes forcefully, but they still share.* It is the duty of a parent or grandparent to teach and train children to share. It really never becomes second nature. Even adults are selfish.
Romans 12:10 - "Be kindly affectioned one to another with brotherly love; in honour preferring one another."
Ask yourself, "Am I a selfish person? Am I willing to share what I have preferring one another?"

5.   *Toddlers memorize quickly.* While traveling in the car or swinging in the swing, I quote Bible verses and sing Bible songs to our grandkids. They remember what we say to them; therefore, it is important to pour God's Word into their hearts.

Psalm 119:11 - "Thy word have I hid in mine heart, that I might not sin against thee." You may not be able to quickly memorize things anymore, but ask yourself, "Do I work at memorizing God's Word at all?

6.   *Toddlers think sharply.* A child can remember going to a restaurant, where they sat and what they ate. They have sharp minds because their little minds are not pulled in so many directions.

Isaiah 26:3 - "Thou wilt keep him in perfect peace, whose mind is stayed on thee: because he trusteth in thee."

Ask yourself, "How do I use my mind? Am I using my mind to think of what God would have me to?"

7.   *Toddlers connect their heart willingly.* It is so easy to win the heart of a child. Play with them, read to them, listen to them and ask them questions. They will give you their heart because you make an investment in them personally.

Proverbs 23:26 - "My son, give me thine heart."

Ask yourself, "What or who is my heart willingly connected to? Have I willingly given my heart to God?"

8.   *Toddlers repeat unnecessarily.* Children repeat what they have heard and seen. It's their natural instinct to do so. They repeat what we teach them. When you play hide and seek with them, they will hide where you hid when it is their turn. They use the tone of voice that you use when looking for them.

Psalm 34:13 - "Keep thy tongue from evil, and thy lips from speaking guile."

Ask yourself, "Is what I am saying okay to be repeated? Can my words and my life be repeated by my children or grandchildren?"

9.   *Toddlers operate simply.* Their lives are not complicated. They operate best on a simple schedule. They do the necessary; therefore, their minds are free to learn, and their hearts are free to give.
Micah 6:8 - "He hath shewed thee, O man, what is good; and what doth the Lord require of thee, but to do justly, and to love mercy, and to walk humbly with thy God?"
Our lives would be less cluttered if we would live by the principles of this verse. Ask yourself, "Do I simply live by the Word of God and operate accordingly?"

10.   *Toddlers trust fully.* They feel safe and secure in the care of a loving parent or grandparent, fully trusting them. Proverbs 3:5-6 - "Trust in the LORD with all thine heart; and lean not unto thine own understanding. In all thy ways acknowledge him, and he shall direct thy paths."
Ask yourself, "Do I fully trust God with my family, my finances, and my future?"

What can you learn from a toddler? Let's all listen and learn, for the Bible clearly teaches that Jesus loves the "little ones." Truths from toddlers are lessons for life!

Pause to Ponder

_____
_____
_____
_____
_____
_____
_____
_____
_____
_____
_____
_____
_____
_____
_____
_____
_____
_____
_____
_____
_____
_____

The Elevator Concept

Revelation 3:15-16
"I know thy works, that thou art neither cold nor hot:
I would thou wert cold or hot. So then because
thou art lukewarm, and neither cold nor hot,
I will spue thee out of my mouth."

Have you ever had an elevator door close on you? If it was an older elevator, the door might have closed on your arm, your leg or half your body. The bottom line is that you were not all in. Because you were not all in, the elevator was not operable. The elevator could not operate until you were all in or all out!

When our children were young, just about any elevator that our family rode on, my husband would put his hands on both doors and push the doors open with all his strength, and our kids thought their Dad was the strongest man in the whole world! The elevator could not operate until the doors were freed from "the strongest dad in the world."

Matthew 15:1-20 describes a group of people who were not all in: the Scribes and Pharisees. They had religion, but they didn't have a relationship with Jesus. They had traditions, but they did not enjoy time with the Savior. The Scribes and Pharisees didn't get it. They didn't understand. They chose not to be teachable. They were not all in. I encourage you to read these verses with the thought of being all in. What lessons can be learned from this group of religious people?

All refers to the whole quantity. An even better meaning of all is the old saying, "All means all and that's all that all can mean." The meaning of in is used to indicate location or position within something. It is easy to consider my body being all in the elevator; however, it's a different thought to consider if I am all in on a spiritual level. Let's consider a few areas of being all in:

1.   Be all in spiritually. You must have a close walk with the Lord if you are going to be a spiritual Christian. A spiritual Christian grows in Christ, walks with Him daily and desires His will to be done in their lives. Remember, you cannot be spiritual if you do not develop a spiritual appetite. Be all in!

2.   Be all in motivationally. Be motivated about serving Christ in your local church.

What can you accomplish for Christ through the ministry that God has allowed you to participate in? Do your part from the bottom of your heart and with everything you have! Give all! Be all in!

3.   Be all in concerning your leadership. Every one of us leads someone. Who do you lead? The children in your Sunday School Class? Your own children? Your grandchildren? Your co-workers? Don't be afraid to stand up for what you believe and Who you believe in. Be all in!

4.   Be all in concerning your "inreach." People in your local church need you. Get to know someone that you do

not know. Be their friend. Reach out to them. Pray for them. Love them. Encourage them. Be all in!

5. Be all in concerning your outreach. Tell people about Jesus. Each of us has a testimony if we have been born again. Give a gospel tract to people whose paths you cross. Never be ashamed to stand for Christ. He died for our sins and rose again that we might go to Heaven to be with Him! Be all in!

Almost every Sunday I ride the elevator at our church with some of our grandchildren. One pushes the button on the outside to call the elevator. We enter the elevator, and then another pushes the button inside to tell the elevator to go down to the first floor. Every time we ride all of us completely get on the elevator. Why? Because the elevator doesn't operate unless we are all in.

Do you live by the elevator concept? Are you all in?

Pause to Ponder

_____

_____

_____

_____

_____

_____

_____

_____

_____

_____

_____

_____

_____

_____

_____

_____

_____

_____

_____

_____

_____

_____

_____

_____

Day 31

Watch Your Step

Job 18:7
*"The steps of his strength shall be straitened, and his
own counsel shall cast him down."*

It is so sweet watching a baby learning to walk. I remember when our children learned to take their first steps. Pulling up to a chair, letting go for a few seconds, turning and taking a couple of steps before falling down, trying over and over again, until finally…there they went, stretching the band of independence a bit more.

We were so excited to see them blossom in this new venture of life. They felt so big, so free, so independent. Once a toddler learns to walk, they begin to follow you around. Wherever you go, they want to be there also. You soon learn that they are trying to step exactly where you make your steps. Your child looks at you and wants to be like you, going wherever you are going and doing whatever you are doing.

I'm sure all of us have carefully directed our steps as we knew those young eyes were watching and those steps were following. I find myself doing the same training with our grandkids, better known as my "Cute Kids." When

116

crossing the street or a parking lot, we hold hands and say, "Look both ways." "Let's wait for that car." "Look to your left; now look to your right." Why do we do that? Because we don't want to get hit by an oncoming vehicle, and we don't want our kids to get hit by an oncoming vehicle. It's simply teaching safety.

I'm reminded of the hymn "Footsteps of Jesus" as I consider this thought:
"Sweetly, Lord, have we heard Thee calling,
Come, follow Me!
And we see where Thy footprints falling
Lead us to Thee.
Footprints of Jesus,
That make the pathway glow;
We will follow the steps of Jesus
Where'er they go."

The instructions are so simple, we follow in the footsteps of Christ and others follow in our footsteps until they understand how to follow in the footsteps of Christ. I don't want to lead anyone to walk out in front of a car. Neither do I want to endanger anyone on the spiritual path. I must watch my steps physically and spiritually.

We are reminded in I Peter 2:21: "For even hereunto were ye called: because Christ also suffered for us, leaving us an example, that ye should follow his steps:"

Teaching our children the concept of walking, we begin by holding both hands, leading them. Then, they have some balance, and we only hold one hand, leading them. After they get the walking concept, they don't want to hold our hands at all because they love being able to get around all by themselves. "Myself," I can hear them say. So, we begin to lead by saying, "No" to the stairs or certain rooms that might not be supervised at the moment. We do this because we are giving them an example by what we say and do.

It's really that simple spiritually. The most difficult part is giving up our selfish, stubborn ways so that we can submissively follow His steps.

Whose steps are you walking in? And who is walking in your steps? Will you step up so that someone can spiritually follow your steps? Watch your step! Someone is following you!

Pause to Ponder

G.L.U.E.

Romans 15:5-6
*"Now the God of patience and consolation grant you to
be likeminded one toward another according to Christ
Jesus: That ye may with one mind and one mouth glorify
God, even the Father of our Lord Jesus Christ."*

"I glued it back together," Mama will say. My mom can
fix anything with a little bit of glue. She believes in that
stuff. She will try to glue anything at least once. One of
her foundational statements is, "Doctors even use glue
to close up a person after surgery." We have laughed for
many years about Mama and her glue, but the truth is, I'm
a little like her myself. Glue is awesome stuff!

What is it about glue? It's such an inexpensive product,
yet it is needed and used by everyone. It is used for crafts,
and it is used for necessities. It is the ingredients that
make glue so special. Glue is simply an adhesive sub-
stance used for sticking objects or materials together. Certain types of glues are stronger than others. There is an
infomercial that is so funny to me because it is advertised
as sticking heavy objects together immediately. It probably works, and if it were cheap enough, I might just order
some and try it out.

Through the years, I have learned a secret about gluing stuff together. There must be proper pressure applied in the right areas for the glue to work. For example, you can glue a picture frame back together at the corners, but if you don't apply pressure on those corners, the frame remains broken.

As a mom, I'm always looking for glue to hold our family together. It takes the ingredients of family glue along with proper pressure for the glue to take hold. This is not a new philosophy for me. As our family grew from 2 to 3 to 4 to 5, it was important that we all enjoy being together and look forward to special times planned with each other. Then, as our family grew from 5 to 6 to 7 to 8, family emphasis remained a priority. Now with 7 "Cute Kids" in our lives, what another family depth to grow through and experience! It is my desire for our family to be held together by the strongest glue possible as we are now 4 distinct families, yet we are also a whole. Let's look at an acrostic to help you think of glue possibilities for your family.

Give of your time, talents and treasures. It takes all three mixed with a giving spirit for family to gain from being together. Give of your time to plan activities and meals. Give of your talents to use your resources for quality conversation. Give of your treasures as you get a minute here or there. Do something age appropriate and give of your time, talents and treasures.

Love unconditionally. It doesn't matter how your spouse, your child, your in-law, or your grandchildren respond to you; it matters how you respond to them. Jesus loves us unconditionally. He loves people who are very different than He is. He accepts us even though we are selfish, unlovable, and not accepting of others by nature. Let's unconditionally love the people we love the most. Placing conditions on our love causes us to be partial toward some family members. This is noticeable and very hurtful to other family members, thus resulting in a breakdown in the family glue. Want a close family? Apply unconditional love.

Understand the perspective of the other family members. The way you do something is not the only way it can be done. Remind yourself that your husband and you were not reared in the same home. Your sons- and daughters-in-law were not reared in your home. Pick up a few new tips that will help you to do something fresh. Understanding the ones who make up the family you love is an ingredient in family glue that holds hearts together and touches lives in a real and loving manner.

Enjoy time together. It is easy to plan time to be together, to spend money for a meal, to work diligently on the plans, and then, to be so busy and distant when family time comes that you don't enjoy any quality time at all. Talk, laugh, listen, and learn your family individually and as a whole, for enjoyment is an ingredient in family glue that is a lasting hold!

There are so many other words that could fit in the acrostic of G.L.U.E. What are the ingredients in the glue that holds your family together? What makes your G.L.U.E. special? Write them down and continually work on your family G.L.U.E.!

Pause to Ponder

A Family Thought

Luke 11:17
"But he, knowing their thoughts, said unto them, Every kingdom divided against itself is brought to desolation; and a house divided against a house falleth."

My husband and I had a most memorable vacation a few years ago. The first segment was spent on Mackinac Island in Michigan. The second segment was at a wedding in Ohio of a young man from our church, and, the third segment was at a quaint town named Frankenmuth in Michigan. All three of these segments were very different from each other and diverse in style; yet, they all had one common thread—family! The island, the wedding and the small town were filled with family-oriented activities and businesses.

I enjoyed the story of the family who owns much of Mackinac Island, how they greet the horses each afternoon at the end of the day and how this family-owned business is totally involved in the day-to-day activities of the island. The wedding was emotionally touching as I watched two sets of parents give away their children in such a godly manner. The ceremony was God-honoring, and both families were pleased that their child had found a godly mate.

I was also touched with the story of a man who owned the riverboat in Frankenmuth. He and his two sons ran the boat along with the grandkids. It was touching to watch them work together and talk about the business. Their kindness to their customers and to each other as well as their ownership of this small business was so sweet.

As I began to notice this common thread that week, it made me think about who really knows and understands me best. That's family. The family unit was designed by God for the purpose of having close, intimate relationships. The family should support each other in bad times and in good times. They should be there for each other through thick and thin.

The devil really wants to destroy the family. It is his goal to divide, splinter, break up and diversify each and every family unit possible. I can understand why the devil would like to accomplish this goal, but I cannot understand why we, as Christians, line up to help him do so.

Some of you reading this devotional are not from a strong family heritage, but you have the opportunity to begin that heritage for your children. Some of you are from a very strong heritage, but you are allowing the devil to destroy your present family. Some of you are carrying on the family heritage in a strong manner.

1. Make a list of traditions that will strengthen your family.
2. Be teachable as your family reveals to you truths about yourself that are inconsistent or ungodly.
3. Determine that your family will have a strong Christian heritage.
4. Remember that God created the family unit and He wants you to thrive and be happy within those boundaries.

I will have to admit that a few times during our trip I said,

"Wish the kids could see this." It is my desire that our family will be first strong in spiritual commitment and second strong in traditions, so that we can continue to grow as the family unit that God intended.

This is just a family thought!

Pause to Ponder

Role Play or Real Relationship?

Jude 21
"Keep yourselves in the love of God, looking for the mercy of our Lord Jesus Christ unto eternal life."

"Dr. Nana," I can hear one of my grandkids say, "My sweetheart needs you." Role play is immediate upon hearing the voice of one of my Cute Kids. Immediately, I stop what I'm doing to take care of the need of the moment. I put concern in my voice, check the tongue, feel the forehead, see if their knees will bend, and then comes the cure. I blow on their tummy, or "sugar bowl" as I regularly call it. This brings laughter which lets them know that they are cured! My role as Dr. Nana is a 24/7 calling. Why do I immediately respond? Because the relationship that I have with my grandkids is very special and important to me. I want to play with them, talk to them, and interact with them because my desire is that our relationship grows stronger by being together.

Role play is not real; however, it produces a real, living relationship. It has a purpose and giving myself wholly to that purpose produces results. It is not the role play that produces true results; it is the personal response and desired relationship with the children that I love so very much. That's what it is all about.

Thinking about this role play brings to mind my relationship with God, my Heavenly Father. When He calls, I can't help but ask myself, "Do I immediately respond?" Do I desire to have an interactive and responsive relationship with God like I do with my Cute Kids? Role play has no good merit, spiritually speaking. Instead, it is a real relationship with God that we must desire to have.

Being interactive with God is pursued through reading His Word and responding to what He speaks to you about.

In Philippians 1:3-11, Paul told these Christians that he thanked God for them and that he prayed for them consistently. He reminded these people whom he loved so much that he knew God was going to work in and through them. Paul said that he had them in his heart. He prayed that their love and knowledge would grow. He wanted things to be excellent in their lives.

What a wonderful example of true Christianity. There is no role play represented here. Is your relationship with Christ real? Genuine? Sincere? Is it loving and excellent? Do you respond to Christ immediately, desiring to please Him with your response and reaction?

I have a real relationship with each of my children and grandchildren. I desire for that individual relationship to grow stronger and deeper by the day and continue to grow for a lifetime. It is more important that my relationship with God continue to grow deeper and stronger; growing and thriving with excellence until I see Him face to face.

Ask yourself, "Am I role playing with Christ or do I have a real relationship?" Seek to grow your relationship with your loved ones and with Christ today!

Pause to Ponder

That's My Stuff!

I John 2:15
"Love not the world, neither the things that are
in the world. If any man love the world,
the love of the Father is not in him."

"That's my stuff, Nana," I hear Cute Kid #3 say over and again. Aubrey discovered a plastic hamburger container and claimed it as her space. "That is your stuff" is my response. Aubrey Grace was two years old at the time. She had discovered stuff. I expect that from a two-year-old, and I don't allow another child to come in and take it without permission. She has claimed her territory for that particular period of playtime.

"That's my stuff," I say every now and then. I just can't get rid of it or do without my stuff. But, why does stuff mean so much to me? It can't love me, it can't provide for me, it can't satisfy me, it is just there, pretending to fill a need but truly cannot fill the desire of my heart. Stuff is a false filler for a true need that each of us have in our lives. Stuff is a façade that we often use to prevent the revealing of our true selves. We hide behind stuff such as clothing, jewelry, makeup, shoes, a nice home, a good education, collections of some kind, and sometimes, just simply piles of stuff. We keep stuff as a security blanket, and we often behave like a two-year-old concerning our collections.

What kind of stuff do you collect? It's easy to collect physical, emotional, and spiritual stuff. Our lives are cluttered, complicated and simply filled with collections of stuff that is confusing our everyday lives.

First, let's get over our physical stuff. It is a good testimony to have a clean home and an organized kitchen. When uncleanness or a messy home takes over our lives preventing us from truly using our home for God's glory, then it becomes a stumbling block. The Bible is clear in its declaration to us in Philippians 4:19, "But my God shall supply all your need according to his riches in glory by Christ Jesus." There is no need in holding on to stuff, when God plainly tells us that He will supply what we need.

Next, let's get over our emotional stuff. Often times we hang on to past hurts and failures. We hold grudges and live under the influence of our past. Instead, we must move forward past the emotional stuff that prefers to crowd our lives. Each of us has someone to forgive. Each of us has something to forget. Let's get over the emotional stuff that clutters our present lives so that we may fill our days with God's purpose. Philippians 3:13-14 are clear: "Brethren, I count not myself to have apprehended: but this one thing I do, forgetting those things which are behind, and reaching forth unto those things which are before, I press toward the mark for the prize of the high calling of God in Christ Jesus." The question is, "Are you forgetting what you should forget? Are you reaching forth to what you should reach for?"

Finally, let's get over our spiritual stuff. We choose whether we are living a spirit-filled or carnal-filled life. I Peter 2:5 challenges us to be a spiritually growing and thriving Christian: "Ye also, as lively stones, are built up a spiritual house, an holy priesthood, to offer up spiritual sacrifices, acceptable to God by Jesus Christ."

Stay in church, do the right things, read God's Word, and be whom God wants you to be!

That's my stuff; but what kind of stuff am I collecting?

Pause to Ponder

An Important Part of Motherhood

Isaiah 66:13
*"As one whom his mother comforteth, so will I comfort
you; and ye shall be comforted in Jerusalem."*

I love to play Peter Pan with our grandchildren. We swing
pretending to fly to the second star to the right and straight
on 'til morning. We play on a fort at a park pretending to
be on Captain Hook's pirate ship. We watch Peter as he
gets his shadow sewn back on with a needle and thread by
Wendy. Then, Wendy and her brothers are sprinkled with
pixie dust and off they fly to Never Land with Peter so that
the lost boys can have a mother to tell them stories.

Everyone needs a mother. Not a mother in name only, but
a true, godly mother, dedicated to the teaching and training of her children. Being a mother is descriptive in so
many ways. Good story telling is one of the joys that a
mother should participate in with her precious little ones.
When our children were in the home, I always tried to tell
some kind of true life story from my childhood or from
their childhood right before bedtime. I always looked forward to this time each evening.

The purpose of storytelling is to bond your heart with the

heart of your child! When bonding happens from the inside out, many things are accomplished in the life of the parent and the child. Mothers, you carry much responsibility in the bonding process. The purpose of bonding hearts with your child is so that you will not lose them spiritually.

During your time of storytelling, make sure that you include a few key principles.

1. Talk about the importance of daily devotions.
2. Be openly affectionate with proper touch and saying "I love you."
3. Include stories about answered prayer.
4. Use third-party teaching, which is simply stories that happened to others.
5. During this time, never belittle or undermine others or your children.
6. Compliment your children on inner beauty.
7. Include how much God loves them and that it is an unconditional love.
8. Comfort your child with your words and through your actions.
9. Talk about the Holy Spirit and how God sent His Son into the world to die for our sins and He sent the Holy Spirit to live within you once you are saved.
10. Be open and honest with your child on their level of understanding.

Our verse for today reminds us that God is our comforter. He wants to comfort you, protect you, guide you, listen to you, help you and love you just as a mother should be all of those things for her child. A mother may let you down, but God never will! Jesus spoke these words of comfort: "And I will pray the Father, and he shall give you another Comforter, that he may abide with you for ever." (Jn. 14:16) ·

"But the Comforter, which is the Holy Ghost, whom the

Father will send in my name, he shall teach you all things, and bring all things to your remembrance, whatsoever I have said unto you." (Jn. 14:26)

"But when the Comforter is come, whom I will send unto you from the Father, even the Spirit of truth, which proceedeth from the Father, he shall testify of me:" (Jn. 15:26)

"Nevertheless I tell you the truth; It is expedient for you that I go away: for if I go not away, the Comforter will not come unto you; but if I depart, I will send him unto you." (Jn. 16:7)

Be comforted through the Holy Spirit and share your comfort through motherhood!

Pause to Ponder

My Emotional Heart

Jeremiah 32:39
"And I will give them one heart, and one way, that they
may fear me for ever, for the good of them, and of their
children after them:"

Riley, our oldest grandchild, told her cousin Owen: "Owen, my heart was so sad yesterday." I listened intently as this 5-year-old shared her heart with her cousin, who is 3 months younger in age. How did Riley know to say, "My heart is sad"? I don't know, but I do know that each of us has 2 kinds of hearts: the heart that pumps blood and the heart that feels emotion.

"I love you with all my heart," you may say. Or you may say, "In your heart, you know that what I'm saying is true." What about, "My head told me one thing, but my heart told me another."

Idioms are also used regularly by you and me. "Cross my heart," meaning to tell the truth, is an often-used idiom. Another is, "That does my heart good," meaning I'm happy about the information I've just heard. I might say that "I know a song by heart" meaning that I have it memorized. One of my favorites is, "You are a person after my own heart," meaning that you feel or think the same thing about a situation.

The Bible speaks about our heart. God made us emotional beings. He knows that we are up and down. We are capable of feeling sad and happy. We can laugh or cry, hurt or heal from the hurt. Because of how God made us, He allows us to choose what we do with our emotions. We can control them, or they can control us. Through our emotional ups and downs, God would have us to make good and godly choices so that our heart remains in a state of spiritual growth. God wants to use you and me through each emotional trial.

God gives us specifics concerning our heart in Ezekiel 36:26-27: "A new heart also will I give you, and a new spirit will I put within you: and I will take away the stony heart out of your flesh, and I will give you an heart of flesh. And I will put my spirit within you, and cause you to walk in my statutes, and ye shall keep my judgments, and do them."

You and I can have a heart of stone. A stone cannot be molded into something else. It's a hard, unmovable rock that will not bend. It is not able to be used as anything except for a hard stone. The Bible tells us that my heart and your heart can be like a stone.

Ask yourself these questions, "Do I have a stony heart that is filled with pride?" Pride simply says that my way is the right way. "Do I have a stony heart that is filled with guilt?" Guilt keeps you and me from trusting God and moving on. The third question to ask is, "Do I have a stony heart of being unteachable?" Not being teachable prevents me from serving God like He wants you to serve Him.

Ask yourself today, "Do I have an emotional heart of stone or of flesh?" Give your emotional heart to God and allow Him to mold it into a beautiful heart of flesh!

Pause to Ponder

The Heart Affects the Outcome

Luke 24:31-32
"And their eyes were opened, and they knew him;
and he vanished out of their sight. And they said
one to another, Did not our heart burn within us,
while he talked with us by the way, and while he
opened to us the scriptures?"

I love to decorate and celebrate every season of the year. When my heart gets involved, the outcome of my plans is going to be good. The more my heart is affected, the more the season I'm preparing for is emphasized in our home. Why? Because my heart affects the outcome of my décor, my plan, my involvement, my life.

I love simple decorations for the spring. Changing the wreath on the front door and being outside more is so refreshing. I even enjoy spring cleaning! It excites me to think about the days having more daylight so we can enjoy the outdoors longer. Spring brings warmer weather, which means that I can get outside with my grandkids and enjoy time with them. However, it's not the spring season, but instead the people behind my thoughts that excite me to prepare for spring.

Summer is another favorite. I love summer days to be home, to have the grandkids come over and play in the sprinkler, and to take late evening walks. It's not really about summer, but it's about the people that I am able to enjoy during the summer months that make me want to put my time and efforts into summer preparation.

Fall has become one of my favorite seasons to decorate for. It is also a favorite because I love going to the NC State Fair and the pumpkin farm with our family. Again, it's not the decorating and events, but the people behind them that make me want to get it going for the season.

Christmas was the season that was the most decorated for and celebrated in our home while I was growing up. I loved to wake up on Christmas morning to the smell of the gas heater and peek in the living room to see if "Santa" had come during the night. Sure enough, he had come and delivered presents wrapped in red paper. I loved that paper. There was something calming about its familiarity. It was always the same kind year after year. Now I know that Daddy got it from the textile mill where he worked. My enjoyment of Christmas as a child put a yearning in me to love the season and to build upon the foundation of tradition that I had received. When I think about the overwhelming amount of work that goes into decorating for Christmas, I turn my focus to the people that I will interact with during the season, and it puts a burning within my heart to get it done and to enjoy it. It's not about the décor, the parties or the busyness. The reason I enjoy the Christmas season so much is the people.

As I mention these seasons, something inside me begins to build. My heart beats a bit stronger, my energy begins to build, my mind begins to think, and I just want to begin the process for whichever season it is. Why is that? Because the process of preparing for each season reminds me of the people that I will interact with during that time.

143

I use the illustrations of seasons to build the thought of the Person who keeps our heart through the seasons of life. That Person is Jesus Christ. Every day, every activity, every season, everything we do should be with a heart to serve Jesus. When I consider what I can do or am about to do for Christ, my heart should begin to beat a bit stronger, my energy level should begin to build, my mind should begin to think of the opportunities I have to serve Him and my excitement should be off the chart!

1. Study God's Word more and with more desire and passion to know Him! Jim Berg eloquently explains, "It is studying the Bible to learn more about a Person – God Himself. The principles you find along the way are manifestations of His Character. If you don't see the Person behind the principles, you have missed God's intention for His revelation." Knowing God more intimately will lead to some practices in your life.

2. Praise God with a more genuine, heartfelt praise. Philippians 4:4 commands, "Rejoice in the Lord always: and again I say, Rejoice." Praise the Lord as you shop. Praise the Lord for your church. Praise the Lord through trials. The saying goes, "If we praised God more, we would have more to praise God for."

3. Practice patience in your everyday life. James 5:8 offers a timely reminder: "Be ye also patient; establish your hearts: for the coming of the Lord draweth nigh." God is so forbearing with us. He waits patiently as we prolong what we know to do for Him. He is longsuffering as we pass up another opportunity to be a witness for Him. He is so patient with us, yet we are so impatient with others. Each season of our lives brings some kind of change. Get rid of the "it's-all-about-me" syndrome. It's really all about God. As you and I search to know God more, we will see Him and practice His love as we are patient with the people we love the most.

4. Prioritize prayer, remembering that conversation is never one-sided with your best friend. Philippians 4:6 exhorts, "Be careful for nothing; but in every thing by prayer and supplication with thanksgiving let your requests be made known unto God." Pray instead of worry. Everything will come together. Has worry ever helped a situation in your life? No. So, pray instead. Pray that your plans please the Lord. Pray that your family will grow closer to each other through the experience that you provide. Pray that you can be a Christian example for those who notice how you celebrate holidays. Pray at meal time, using this opportunity to touch the lives of those in your home.

5. Live a peaceful life. Philippians 4:7 promises, "And the peace of God, which passeth all understanding, shall keep your hearts and minds through Christ Jesus." Peace is the result of the Person of God, praising Him, patience with others, and communication with God through prayer. Every home can have peace. It doesn't take money, nice décor or big plans. Peace is not explainable because it is of God. The Bible says peace that "passeth all understanding." Peace is one of those attributes that you cannot touch, but you know when you have it. Peace will keep your heart. The word *keep* refers to spiritual stability. Have you ever said, "I think I'm going to lose my mind"? That means that at that time we were not practicing the peace of God. You are actually trying to handle the situation on your own.

How is your heart? It's an important question because your heart affects your outcome!

Pause to Ponder

Embrace His Shadow

Psalm 17:8
"Keep me as the apple of the eye,
hide me under the shadow of thy wings."

Many times I have taken my hand and shielded a child's eyes from the sun. It only takes a bump, and my hand moves. The sun immediately shines brightly in the child's face, causing him to cry or complain. The shadow of my hand can only protect a child from the sun in a small degree. When a child embraces the shadow, it is helpful to his comfort.

A shadow of a tree brings shade to a person, a car, or anything in its path. It protects from the direct rays of the sun. How many times have you chosen a parking spot because of the shade of a tree? Embracing the shadow of a tree enhances comfort when returning to your car as well as protects the outer surface of the vehicle.

Have you ever been talking to someone and the sun was shining directly in your eyes? What did you do? You stood in their shadow so that your eyes were protected. You could see the person, and your eyes didn't pour water. As long as you stayed in their shadow, conversation was good. When you moved out of their shadow, you had to turn your face away in order to continue conversation. Why? Embracing the shadow of the person brought protection from the sun and added comfort to your conversation.

On the flip side, sometimes a shadow can be a frightful thing. Children are especially fearful of shadows. They need assurance that everything is okay. This protective security is needed in the life of a child. More than a shadow, there can be strange and frightful things that come into each of our lives.

The Bible talks about God's shadow and how it benefits His children. "I have put my words in thy mouth, and I have covered thee in the shadow of mine hand, that I may plant the heavens, and lay the foundations of the earth, and say unto Zion, Thou art my people." (Is. 51:16)

God is big enough to cover you in the shadow of His hand. He can cover you and me at the same time. His desire is for your life to be joyful, depending upon Him all the way. When you follow His plan for your life, when you say what He wants you to say, when you don't know what to do or where to turn, no worries, you are in the shadow of His hand! God's hand never moves so much that His shadow is not where you need it to be. God's protection is with you, His child. Embrace His shadow!

Pause to Ponder

Learning to Let Go

Isaiah 43:18-19
"Remember ye not the former things, neither consider the things of old. Behold, I will do a new thing; now it shall spring forth; shall ye not know it? I will even make a way in the wilderness, and rivers in the desert."

One of the most difficult things to do is to let go. Letting go of anything, really. Letting go of an old shirt that you have become attached to. Letting go of the way you've always done it. Letting go of a car upon trade-in because you feel like you are betraying it. And, one of the most difficult challenges is letting go of your child when they have reached the end of high school and are moving on to the next phase of their growing up life. All of these statements are true for me, but reaching the end of my teaching and training with our children upon high school graduation was a tough, emotional struggle for me. Wondering what the future held for home life without all of my babies home; wondering if life would ever have the same feeling and meaning; wondering if we had truly done our job to the best of our ability; wondering if they were ready to face the world without mom or dad helping them on a daily basis; and so many more questions came to my mind.

Our children are married with children now, and we have survived the process of letting go on several levels. There was a time when I believed that I had "cut the apron strings" as the old adage goes. Then, I realized that there were all kinds of fishing lines attached. As I have continued to clip the invisible attached strings, I have learned some things along the way. We were a close family in the growing up years, and we continue to have closeness in each stage of life. We were a family that did things together. We continue to work at being a together family by continuing established traditions and establishing new ones.

Whether you are the parent of a child leaving, the child who has grown up, or the in-law that has just joined the family, there are a few things to consider as you let go to move forward in the life that God has waiting for you.

1. Be willing to change. Change is difficult, but change can be a good thing. Half the battle is resolved when you are willing to change.

2. Prepare for change. The first step in preparation is mental. Deal with the fact that you are not losing your child; you are allowing him/her to become what you have prayed for. Put this mental challenge into physical reality.

3. Celebrate the past by remembering. As our children were growing up, I kept a video tape running for them individually. After they were married, I had their series of videos made into DVD's and gave them their set for Christmas one year. This was a letting-go process for me. I love to look at old pictures or videos, but I cannot live there. God never intended it to be that way. Your children enjoy remembering with you if you are able to move on.

4. Celebrate the future by preparing. Grandkids have been such a fun future for us. It helped me to prepare each of my kid's rooms with their wedding pictures and add

their children's picture to their room. Prepare by using the past to have an exciting present.

Consider the verse for today. Life changes. If you are reading this devotion, then it means that you have life. God is not finished with you yet. He wants to do a new thing in you. God wants to give new life, new happiness. He wants to make a way in the wilderness. He wants to give you water if you are in the desert. Sometimes things do not turn out the way we planned. It's difficult to let go because things are not so good. God wants to use you still. He wants you to grow from the former things to new things. God is in control of your present. Let go and allow Him to be in control of your life!

I think of Mary and how hard it must have been for her to see Jesus hanging on the cross. I am thankful she let go, aren't you? I think of Hannah, and how she prayed for a child. She promised God that if He would allow her to have a son, she would give him for God's service very young. She did that by giving Samuel to be Eli's helper in the temple at a young age. What a sacrifice! Our children are given to us for a short period of time for training and for preparing them for life. Learn to let go and let God work!

Pause to Ponder

The Heart of the Matter

Proverbs 23:19
"Hear thou, my son, and be wise,
and guide thine heart in the way."

In today's society, children seem to be a liability to many people. This world is filled with people who have children, but do not want to be parents. Parents swallow the new idea that quality time is better than quantity time. Parents have also been influenced by the new idea that incentives produce more than authority. You must not be embarrassed or afraid to be an authority in your child's life.

Proverbs 4:23 says, "Keep thy heart with all diligence; for out of it are the issues of life." The heart determines behavior. The behavior you or your child exhibits is an expression of the overflow of the heart. Mark 7:21 tells us that evil thoughts come outwardly as an overflow of the heart.

You must not just understand the "what" of your child's actions, you must understand the "why." You must show them by leading, not just by instruction. Their thoughts must be guided, helping them to learn wisdom and discernment. You must invest your life in your child, participating in open and honest communication. Your goal cannot simply be well-behaved children; it must be understanding why your child did what they did. Centralize your focus around the Bible; after all, it is our hands-on guide.

Ask yourself these questions:
1. Does my child need more positive attention from me?
2. Does my child need a balance of attention from correction and because of a job well done?
3. Does my child need responsibilities given by me to show I need and approve of his work?
4. Does my child need an opportunity to prove himself?
5. Do I need to brag on my child to them in private?
6. Do I need to brag on my child in public?
7. Do I need to keep the secrets of my child instead of telling my friend?
8. Do I need to be an authority in my child's life instead of a buddy?
9. Do I need to read some good books on parenting and put them into practice?
10. Do I need to understand why my child did what he did instead of seeing only the symptoms of the heart?
11. Do I need to stop questioning authority and start believing that my child is not perfect?

First, evaluate yourself. What do you need to do to improve the heart of the matter? Second, what can your child do? Be the authority and make a difference in the heart of your child. Get to the heart of the matter.

Pause to Ponder

_____

_____

_____

_____

_____

_____

_____

_____

_____

_____

_____

_____

_____

_____

_____

_____

_____

_____

_____

_____

_____

_____

_____

_____

_____

Why?

Psalm 31:24
*"Be of good courage, and he shall strengthen your
heart, all ye that hope in the LORD."*

Children often ask "why." Why is the sun shining? Why
do I have to go to bed? Why do I have to eat my vege-
tables? Even when you give them the answer, the next
question comes, "But, why?" When children are in this
stage of life, there is never an answer that satisfies. Usually children grow out of this stage. Then, they don't have
to ask why because they know everything!

In I Corinthians 1, there are some people in the church
that are in the why stage and possibly the know-it-all
stage. These people were asking questions and having
opinions that were similar to children.

Read I Corinthians 1:11-18 and listen to what these people are saying. Try to hear their tone of voice.
"For it hath been declared unto me of you, my brethren,
by them which are of the house of Chloe, that there are
contentions among you. Now this I say, that every one of
you saith, I am of Paul; and I of Apollos; and I of Cephas;
and I of Christ. Is Christ divided? was Paul crucified for
you? or were ye baptized in the name of Paul? I thank

God that I baptized none of you, but Crispus and Gaius; Lest any should say that I had baptized in mine own name. And I baptized also the household of Stephanas: besides, I know not whether I baptized any other. For Christ sent me not to baptize, but to preach the gospel: not with wisdom of words, lest the cross of Christ should be made of none effect. For the preaching of the cross is to them that perish foolishness; but unto us which are saved it is the power of God."

These verses describe a scene among two church groups, the house of Chloe and the house of Stephanas. Both groups became proud people. They were gloating in who baptized them. This distraction became their focus, and it revealed its root through their foolishness. "Paul baptized me. Who baptized you?" These immature statements and questions were used as a lure from the devil causing the people contention.

You and I can't worship God and stay in His Word as we should when there is contention among us. Silly statements and accusing questions cause contention. Contention causes a lack of focus on the root of what brings us together which is salvation through Jesus Christ, our Savior.

God sent His only Son, Jesus, to die on the Cross for our sins. Our focus should be Jesus, not silly babblings. Do you want to grow spiritually? Then stop the silly statements and accusing questions that cause contention. Some things matter. Ask those questions. Make those statements. Then, move on before contention becomes the distraction. Why? Because Jesus is our focus! He is the root of our joy, and He alone will produce proper fruit in our lives! That's why!

Pause to Ponder

It Takes Time

Ephesians 5:15-16
"See then that ye walk circumspectly, not as fools, but as wise, Redeeming the time, because the days are evil."

On February 19, 2002, at 8:57 AM Central Standard Time, I lost someone dear to my heart. It was my Granny. Not only was she my Granny, but she was called Granny by most people. I remember checking her mail as a child one day, and there was an envelope addressed to: "Granny - Rt. 1, Midland City, Alabama." Even the mailman just knew who she was.

I recall many fun times as a child. Granny seemed to always have time to bake teacakes or Ginger Bread Men– their faces made with raisins. I never did like to eat those men because ginger bread was not good to me, but I loved spending the time making them. I treasure the countless weekends of spending Friday and Saturday night sleeping beside her. Oh, what warmth. And the stories she could tell as we were tightly tucked in together. Warmth, love, security: although I had those things at home with my parents, I still wanted and needed a good, godly grandmother to fill some gaps.

Granny loved to sew. She did not need a pattern, just a newspaper. She made clothes for baby dolls and Barbie dolls. The last one she made for me was in December 2001. She found one of my baby dolls from childhood, cleaned it up, and dressed it beautifully. I treasure it and the others today. Granny also made dresses for us girls to wear for old-fashioned day at church and mascot uniforms for school events. What do all of these things represent? Time. She took time out of her schedule for me, her grandchild.

The Bible clearly speaks about time in our verses for today.
1. Walk circumspectly. Live each day with a constant awareness of the lives you are touching, knowing that each life touched is an investment.
2. Redeem the time. Make spiritual investments in the lives of those you love. Grandparents, take time with your grandchildren. Redeem each opportunity to make a godly impact on those young lives. Why? Because the days are evil, the Bible tells us.

I can hear Granny say to me, "Sharon, I love you. I love all of you." Granny left a note for her family with her funeral instructions. The note concluded, "I loved you all, and I want to see all of you in Heaven one day." These words will live in my heart forever because Granny took the time.

Pause to Ponder

Day 44

You Decide

Joel 3:14
"Multitudes, multitudes in the valley of decision:
for the day of the LORD is near in the valley
of decision."

You make decisions every day. You decide what to wear, what time you leave your house in the morning, which route to take to your destination, how you speak to your family and more. Decisions are a part of all of our lives. Decisions affect our mental being, and they cultivate a right or wrong mental attitude.

The definition of *decide* is to settle; to determine the conclusion of; to make up one's mind. Two people come to mind immediately as I think of the subject of decisions. First, I think of a man named Napoleon, a well-known man who made this statement: "I have never known six happy days in my life." Next, I think of a woman who was blind, deaf, and dumb. Her name was Helen Keller. Although she never saw or heard anything, she made the statement, "I have found life so beautiful." What was the difference between Helen Keller and Napoleon? It was the choice they made of how they would live their life.

My husband has said so many times, "Life is not made up of days; life is made up of decisions." I think of that statement often as I am the only one who chooses decisions that make up every day of my life.

1. Decide to be happy. It is a choice only you can make.
2. Decide to adjust to the circumstances of your world. Helen Keller did.
3. Decide to take care of yourself. You are not a cat with nine lives. You have one body.
4. Decide to strengthen your mind. Read. Be teachable.
5. Decide to exercise your soul. Do what you know to do and be who you know to be.
6. Decide to be agreeable. I am not talking about compromise, just agreeable when it really is just opinion.
7. Decide to live today. Do not borrow from tomorrow or worry about yesterday.
8. Decide to live by a schedule that is based on priorities built upon God's Word. You should not be too busy for God's Work. Remember He gives you the time that you have.
9. Decide to have a quiet time with God each day. It will change your life.
10. Decide not to be afraid to be happy. It is contagious and will affect others.

What decision will you make? You decide.

Pause to Ponder

_____
_____
_____
_____
_____
_____
_____
_____
_____
_____
_____
_____
_____
_____
_____
_____
_____
_____
_____
_____
_____
_____
_____
_____

Guide the House

I Timothy 5:14
"I will therefore that the younger women marry, bear
children, guide the house, give none occasion to the
adversary to speak reproachfully."

The subject of today reminds me of work. The phrase
"guide the house" instructs the woman to be the manager
of the house. It does not say that you are the head, just
the manager. To illustrate this point, let's use the example
of a fast food restaurant. You have the owner, the manager and the employees. The owner gives the orders, but
the manager is the one who carries out those orders and
who keeps the employees working. We've often heard,
"Good, better, best, never let it rest, until your good is
better and your better is best." Choosing to manage your
home is choosing God's best for your life. Romans 12:2
says it well, "And be not conformed to this world: but be
ye transformed by the renewing of your mind, that ye may
prove what is that good, and acceptable, and perfect, will
of God."

In order to be a good home manager, you must be a home
lover. If you carry in your mind the thought "Home Sweet
Home" when referring to your home, you qualify as a

home lover. You must also have the heart of a homemaker. Make homemaking all that it should be. Sometimes we refer to something and say that it is "caught not taught." That is not true with homemaking. It is often "taught not caught."

1.   Plan in detail. Use a planner to write down everything. Do not rely on your memory.
2.   Value each minute. Plan how long a task will take you and work toward that goal.
3.   Keep moving. The principle of momentum: "A body at rest tends to remain at rest, and a body in motion tends to remain in motion.
4.   Develop a routine. Trying to do the same thing at the same time each day conserves and generates energy. It conserves energy by cutting down on indecision. It generates energy through habit.
5.   Ask the "half-the-time" question. "If my life depended on doing this task in half the time, what short cuts would I take?" Then take them.
7.   Do the worst thing first. Once the worst is done, your attitude will greatly improve.
8.   Begin the night before. Plan the next day. Tidy up so you have a positive beginning.
9.   Read on time management. This is time well invested. Constantly work on better use of your time and be organized.
10. Say no. When you do not have time to give, say no. This will keep you from becoming frustrated. This should not be used as an excuse for not being busy for the Lord.

You are the manager of your home. Will you choose today to "guide the house" as God has instructed you to do?

Pause to Ponder

Be a Willing Parent

Psalm 143:10
"Teach me to do thy will; for thou art my God: thy spirit
is good; lead me into the land of uprightness."

"The will of God will not take you where the grace of God will not lead you." In our country church one Sunday morning, my friend and I sang a duet. It was a normal habit for us to sing; however, this particular time seemed so different. In just a few weeks I would be married at the young age of 17 and would move away from the home and church that I had known all of my life. I knew I was headed into the ministry and wasn't sure of all that the ministry had in store. The song we chose to sing was entitled "Whatever It Takes." This song has become a testimonial song for my life as I know God called me away from home to grow spiritually and serve Him with my life.

The Bible reminds us to do the will of God from the heart. "Not with eyeservice, as menpleasers; but as the servants of Christ, doing the will of God from the heart." (Eph. 6:6)

Why did the song touch my heart? Let me quote some of

169

the words for you so that you can understand.

"Take my houses and lands, change my dreams and my plans, for I'm placing my whole life in your hands. And if you call me today to a land far away, Lord I'll go and your will obey.
Take the dearest things to me if that's how it must be, to draw me closer to you. Let the disappointments come, lonely days without the sun, if through sorrow more like you I'll become.
For whatever it takes to draw me closer to you, Lord, that's what I'll be willing to do. For whatever it takes to be more like you. That's what I'll be willing to do...
For whatever it takes for my will to break, that's what I'll be willing to do.
My desire was to do God's will and to serve Him with my life. I've never regretted serving God from my heart!

The Bible also reminds us to obey God's Word. "...we will obey the voice of the LORD our God, to whom we send thee, that it may be well with us, when we obey the voice of the LORD our God." (Jer. 42:6) Many times young people are willing to serve the Lord with their lives. They commit themselves to lifetime service or to do whatever God would have them do, but they have unwilling parents. Their parents have made other plans for the life of their child. Maybe they have planned an unfulfilled dream of their own for their children. Or maybe they push their children into a career of money and prestige. I am sure my parents did not want me to move hundreds of miles away from them, but they were willing parents. Trust God with the life of your child. Remember, your children are a blessing and are on loan to you from God. God has allowed you to train them.

1. God's will is individualized for each one of His children.
2. God will not send you; He will go with you.

170

3. God chooses the available.

Will you allow your child to serve the Lord in His perfect will for their lives? Are you an unwilling parent or a willing parent? I challenge you to examine your heart. Do not be a stumbling block to your children. The will of God will not take you where the grace of God will not lead you. "But the God of all grace, who hath called us unto his eternal glory by Christ Jesus, after that ye have suffered a while, make you perfect, stablish, strengthen, settle you." (I Pet. 5:10) Be a willing parent!

Pause to Ponder

_____
_____
_____
_____
_____
_____
_____
_____
_____
_____
_____
_____
_____
_____
_____
_____
_____
_____
_____
_____
_____
_____

Time for Tea

Colossians 3:15
"And let the peace of God rule in your hearts,
to the which also ye are called in one body;
and be ye thankful."

"Nana, can we have a tea party?" I love those words. "Sure, we can," is my response. Then, off to the kitchen I go to prepare the snacks and tea while the children dress up as their favorite characters. The tea party setting brings quality time, peaceful conversation and interaction.

Did you ever play "tea party" growing up? I did. What fun! When I think of a teapot or a hot cup of tea, I think of peaceful surroundings. I think of the sweet, soothing smell of hot tea. It's easy for me to escape to that frame of mind and leave the hustle, bustle surroundings that are usually present in our day-to-day lives.

The answer to a peaceful life is not found in a teapot or our surroundings. The answer is found in the Bible. Let me encourage you to get your Bible and walk with me through eight principles that lead us to a peaceful life.

1. The Bible tells us to wait on the Lord. (Is. 30:18)

2. The Bible tells us to be content with what we have. (Heb. 13:5)

3. The Bible tells us to have a right spirit. (Ps. 51:10)

4. The Bible tells us to understand what the will of the Lord is. (Eph. 5:6, 7, 11,17)

5. The Bible tells us to get rid of known sin in our lives. (Heb. 12:1-2)

6. The Bible tells us not to worry. (Phil. 4:6-7)

7. The Bible tells us not to be easily offended. (Ps. 119:165)

Ask yourself, "Am I living a peaceful life?" I challenge you to work at it deliberately and daily. Allow the Lord to work peacefully through you!

Pause to Ponder

_____
_____
_____
_____
_____
_____
_____
_____
_____
_____
_____
_____
_____
_____
_____
_____
_____
_____
_____
_____
_____
_____
_____
_____
_____

Day 48

Seeing Through Different Eyes

Mark 8:22-25
"And he cometh to Bethsaida; and they bring
a blind man unto him, and besought him to touch him.
And he took the blind man by the hand, and led him
out of the town; and when he had spit on his eyes,
and put his hands upon him, he asked him if he saw
ought. And he looked up, and said, I see men as trees,
walking. After that he put his hands again upon his eyes,
and made him look up: and he was restored,
and saw every man clearly."

In my personal devotions, I read through the stories of the Bible, a method of reading through the Bible written in the *Christian Life Journal* produced by Dr. Clarence Sexton. This method of reading put each story in the Gospels together so you could compare the personalities of the writers inspired by the Holy Spirit. A particular grouping of miracles caught my attention. That grouping was of the blind men that Jesus chose to heal.

In our reading today, Jesus chose to heal a blind man in the city of Bethsaida. In this particular instance, Jesus' method of healing was to spit on the man's eyes and put his hands on the man. After this first touching, the man looked up and said, "I see men as trees, walking." This sight was better than nothing, but still was not the best sight.

Jesus then put His hands again on the man's eyes and made him look up. This time he saw every man clearly. This was the best sight that the blind man could ask for. He now saw through different eyes.

The miracle was speaking of different eyes physically, but I can't help but to think of different eyes spiritually. It is important as a Christian that you and I have different eyes spiritually.

1. If you have been saved, God has given you new vision, just as the blind man. You now see through different eyes. The old hymn "Amazing Grace" says, "I once was lost but now am found, was blind but now I see." How exciting to know that salvation by grace through faith has given new vision through different eyes.

2. See the future through different eyes.
    a. Make some monthly and yearly goals involving others.
    b. Try to see the outcome of your decisions 10 years down the road.
    c. Unselfishness is only seen through different eyes.

3. See your family through different eyes.
    a. How can I become selfless?
    b. What can I do to improve my relationship with my husband?
    c. Have I given my children wholly to the Lord for Him to use anywhere?
    d. Am I training my children to hear the still small voice of God that they may answer His call to what He would have them to do?
    e. Do I respond to extended family with a sweet spirit?

4. See your friends through different eyes.
    a. Different eyes convict you to talk to others about Christ.
    b. Different eyes see the lost world and stir your heart to do something about it beginning in your own neighborhood.
    c. Different eyes allow you to see a person's heart and motive and not be critical or negative because they are different from you.

Is your vision blurred, or is it as clear as it can be? Allow God to clarify your vision so that you may glorify Him through different eyes.

Pause to Ponder

_____

_____

_____

_____

_____

_____

_____

_____

_____

_____

_____

_____

_____

_____

_____

_____

_____

_____

_____

_____

_____

_____

_____

_____

If You Do Not Go Deep, You Cannot Go High

Colossians 2:7
"Rooted and built up in him, and stablished
in the faith, as ye have been taught,
abounding therein with thanksgiving."

I love the bright sunshine and the long daylight hours of spring and summer. I enjoy working in the yard and seeing new growth on plants. It is refreshing to see the blossoms of new flowers with a wide assortment of colors. There is excitement in looking up at a tall tree that seems so big and lifeless all winter and discover small buds of new growth.

What massive beauty there is in the redwoods. From a seed no bigger than one from a tomato, California's coast redwood may grow to a height of 367 feet and have a width of 22 feet at its base. The roots go down 10 to 13 feet deep before spreading outward 60 to 80 feet. A redwood can grow high because of its deep and wide root system.

The part of spring that is less appreciated is the weeds.

Weeds can grow on the surface and be easily pulled, but some are well rooted. No matter the type of plant, all have roots and grow. However, some plants have deeper roots than others; therefore, they are stronger and can grow taller than the others.

"That Christ may dwell in your hearts by faith; that ye, being rooted and grounded in love, May be able to comprehend with all saints what is the breadth, and length, and depth, and height; And to know the love of Christ, which passeth knowledge, that ye might be filled with all the fulness of God." (Eph. 3:17-19)

Just as a tree cannot grow tall without deep roots, neither can a Christian become more deeply grounded in their Christian faith without going deeper into God's Word. Our foundation must be Christ, for He is the Solid Rock on which to build. Our roots must be planted in the proper soil where they can be nourished. Good Bible preaching and a good local church helps with nourishment. The fertilizer of daily devotions must be added in order to be a strong rooted Christian. The additive of faithful church attendance is a must.

Remember, if you do not go deep, you cannot go high.

Pause to Ponder

_____
_____
_____
_____
_____
_____
_____
_____
_____
_____
_____
_____
_____
_____
_____
_____
_____
_____
_____
_____
_____
_____
_____
_____
_____
_____

Change

Romans 8:27-29
"And he that searcheth the hearts knoweth what
is the mind of the Spirit, because he maketh
intercession for the saints according to the will of God.
And we know that all things work together for good
to them that love God, to them who are the called
according to his purpose. For whom he did foreknow,
he also did predestinate to be conformed
to the image of his Son, that he might be the
firstborn among many brethren."

Change. When I think of that word many things come
to my mind. I think of the little bit of change (money)
returned from teens after a youth activity. I think of how
many times kids have to change clothes during a day because of ball practices and different events taking place in
their lives. High school students change classes. Change
occurs when we lose a loved one. We must adapt to change
when a bad choice has been made, and it effects all who
come in contact with the person who made that choice.
Some change takes place because of the natural process
of life. We all go through the aging process and must accept change. We adjust slowly as our children grow from
infant, to toddler, to young child, to preteen, to teen, to

getting married, to becoming a grandparent.

1.   Change according to God's will. (Rom. 8:27) It is God's will for the natural processes of change to be in our lives. We must not buck the change. "One generation cometh and another generation passeth away"(Ecc. 1:4). It is God's plan for us to adapt to an ever changing family. Kids grow up. Health changes. Generations pass away. How are you adapting to God's will according to the changes taking place in your life?

2.   Change according to God's purpose. (Rom. 8:28) God has an individualized purpose for you and me. He allows change to take place in our lives so that we will purpose it for His glory. Spend a few minutes thinking about God's individualized purpose for your life. Are you using that purpose for God's glory?

3.   Change according to God's conformity. (Rom. 8:29) Whatever change we make in our lives should be progressive toward the being like the image of God's Son. No matter what takes place in our lives, it is to bring us closer to conform to the image of God's son. Consider your life. Is your image conforming more to Christ or conforming more to the world?

Change is going to happen. It is going to take place in each of our lives. Anticipate change so that you can prepare yourself for the future. Think ahead so that you can be as prepared as possible when change occurs. Plan for a change if your family is in a rut. Are changes needed so that the kids want to be home with you? Are you treating them appropriately for their age?

Adapt quickly to the change taking place in your life. The sooner you let go, the sooner you can enjoy the fresh spices of change. If something needs changing in your life, don't just talk about it, do it. Then, seize the moment and enjoy it. By the time you adapt, more change will come so that you can go through the process all over again. As long as we are living on this earth, change will occur. Some changes that we enjoy and some changes that we don't enjoy will confront our lives. It's difficult. It's frightening. It's necessary. Change – it is what you make it!

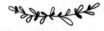

Pause to Ponder

_____
_____
_____
_____
_____
_____
_____
_____
_____
_____
_____
_____
_____
_____
_____
_____
_____
_____
_____
_____
_____
_____
_____

Who Am I?

Luke 10:40-42
*"But Martha was cumbered about much serving,
and came to him, and said, Lord, dost thou not care
that my sister hath left me to serve alone? bid her
therefore that she help me. And Jesus answered and
said unto her, Martha, Martha, thou art careful
and troubled about many things: But one thing
is needful: and Mary hath chosen that good part,
which shall not be taken away from her."*

Many times sisters have opposite personalities, and such was the case with Mary and Martha. They both desired to serve the Lord, but both carried out that serving in a different manner. Did one please the Lord in their serving more than the other one? Yes. Let's look at some possible weaknesses and strengths in each sister.

Martha loved the Lord. She had perfectionist tendencies. Every detail of the meal that Martha was about to serve had to be perfectly carried out. She was so determined to carry out those details that she added tension to the evening. Martha wanted to look good for her Master, so she worked endless hours to make sure the house was in order, the meal was properly prepared and the table was set to perfection. After all, she was doing all of this for

Jesus, and she wanted it to be right. Martha definitely had the gift of hospitality.

Mary loved the Lord. She had a laid-back personality. She also got the job done, but didn't try to do everything at once. Mary did not get caught up in the "do's" of the day, but instead in the people she was serving. Mary was not easily influenced. She was aware of Martha's busyness but did not feel the need for all those things to be done in order to worship Jesus in their home. Mary was not drawn by "do's" as much as the call to worship her Master. Mary had the gift of availability.

Do you have the gift of hospitality or availability? Who do you most identify with, Mary or Martha? I am a Martha. I enjoy staying busy. Usually I make more work than necessary for the day, or plan more for the day than is possible to get accomplished. However, I do desire to worship as Christ would have me to. I must balance work and worship in my life in order to please Christ. You must identify who you are and work on balance as well.

Worship and work are necessary in all of our lives and must be balanced if we are going to serve the Lord effectively. Listed below are a few ideas to help you get started in the right direction toward balancing work and worship.

1.   Identify yourself. Are you a Mary or a Martha?
2.   Do not confuse the urgent with the important. You must prioritize at home, at church and at work.
3.   Use the life of Jesus as your example. Jesus did not live in a hurry. He met the needs of people who were in His path before other duties that He accomplished.
4.   Do not over-commit yourself to duties. Usually being a people-pleaser is the cause of such behavior.
5.   Learn to hear the still small voice of God. He often speaks that way.
6.   Spend the early part of your day in private worship to

God. Daily devotions will help you to prioritize your day putting God first.

7.   Remember that busyness breeds distraction.

8.   If you are a Mary, add some of Martha's qualities.

9.   If you are a Martha, add some of Mary's qualities.

10. Remember that the Bible says in Luke 10:42 – "But one thing is needful: and Mary had chosen that good part, which shall not be taken away from her."

Whether you are a Mary or Martha, begin to work on your weaknesses so that they become your strengths, and be sure to put the Lord first in all that you do today! I'm Martha, trying to add Mary qualities into my life. Who are you?

Pause to Ponder

Spiritual Life Support

Ephesians 6:10-11
"Finally, my brethren, be strong in the Lord,
and in the power of his might. Put on the
whole armour of God, that ye may be able
to stand against the wiles of the devil."

It's often that you hear of someone in the hospital being on life support. The machine is keeping the person alive. It is breathing for them, so that their heart will keep pumping. Usually when the life support system is taken away from the person, that person dies. Why? Because their body was not able to live without life support.

Spiritual Life Support is the same. It is explained as surviving off another person's spirituality. They function pretty normal until a crisis occurs. In the midst of the crisis, they begin to suffer, to become unstable, not realizing that in reality someone else was breathing spiritually for them. It is the plan of the devil for you to be unstable, uncertain as to what you believe, and pulling away from the beliefs that brought you to where you are in your Christian life. Allow me to share with you a true story with the names changed for privacy.

I was talking to a young lady who used to be in our youth

group. She was always a good girl: dependable, fun, loving and a Christian. Brenda's parents got saved later in their lives. Not long after that time, Brenda began attending our Christian school and church. In a church like ours, you can be at church almost any day of the week. The youth group was active, and Brenda was a vital part of it. Brenda wanted to be liked and to fit in with others. She tried to live for the Lord as well as fit in. This affected her spiritual leadership somewhat in the youth group. Brenda went to a Christian college and met a fine young man. They dated, grew to love each other and married. Joseph was also reared in a godly Christian home, a good church and Christian school. Joseph and Brenda continued to serve in our local church after marriage. Brenda expressed to me her innermost feelings, "We were living off of spiritual life support. We had been reared in a Christian home, went to a good church, attended and graduated from a Christian school and Christian college, but did not make those things taught to us real in our lives. They were someone else's rules, convictions, and way of life. We only lived them out pretending they were ours."

Spiritual life support will work for a while, maybe even a few years, but there will come a time in our lives when there must be something more. Our walk with the Lord must be real. We must desire that walk with the Lord. How can that walk be real you may ask? Brenda asked the same question. Now, she knew the answer, just as you probably do, but sometimes we want to make the answer more difficult than it really is. We want to believe that there is more to it than we surely must know or understand. If we are going to be free of "spiritual life support," we must do the things involved in the general will of God:

1. Read your Bible daily. Write down what the Lord has spoken to you about that day. If He doesn't seem to speak to you, read until He does.

2.   Pray daily. Make yourself a prayer journal. Pray for your family daily, then add others—friends, church members, missionaries—different ones each day.

3.   Tell others about the Lord on a regular basis. Be conscious of why the Lord sent you to the place you may be today.

4.   Serve the Lord faithfully in your local church. I love the quote, "We are not saved to sit; we are saved to serve."

5.   Stand for what is right. Dr. Randy Cox, our pastor emeritus, said, "Until you stand and stand and stand, you will not be able to withstand."

When we are faithfully doing God's general will, He will reveal to us His specific will for our lives. True happiness is being in the center of God's will. If you are surviving off of spiritual life support, you cannot and will not continue to grow spiritually. You must put forth the spiritual effort to be strong in the Lord. Ephesians 6:10 tells us, "Finally, my brethren, be strong in the Lord, and in the power of his might." Work those spiritual muscles. God promises to do His part. Joseph and Brenda realized their need to be free of spiritual life support and begin to grow in the Lord on their own. Are you surviving off of spiritual life support?

Pause to Ponder

What's Your Plan?

Psalm 16:5-6
"The LORD is the portion of mine inheritance
and of my cup: thou maintainest my lot.
The lines are fallen unto me in pleasant places;
yea, I have a goodly heritage."

I love a plan! It's exciting to put a plan on paper and then see it through. A plan is a detailed proposal for doing or achieving something; an intention of what one is going to do. My question to you today is, "What is your plan concerning your spiritual heritage?" It's easy to live life, going from event to event and never really have a plan for your future.

Good planners often plan for their children to inherit land, collectibles, money and such upon the passing of parents or loved ones. This is a great plan; however, there is more. These things are temporal. The eternal is most important, and it needs a plan.

It is God's plan that we pass down a godly heritage to our family. You may be a first generation Christian, or you may have many generations of Christianity in your family. Either is a blessing. But, what will you do with your Christian heritage? Will it pass off the scene with you? Do you have plans for your godly heritage to continue?

The Christian bloodline should get stronger from generation to generation. God's plan is for our children, grandchildren and great-grandchildren to put God first in their lives, to trust Him, to remember what He has done, is doing, and will do. Additionally, it is God's plan to pass it on. Anything less affects our joy, our true happiness.

Make plans now for your godly heritage.
1.   Any heritage worth anything is an investment of your time, talent and treasure. It doesn't just happen. Your godly heritage requires investing as well.
2.   Any heritage received has been thought through and written down. Someone doesn't receive a piece of land or a large sum of money unless it has been signed over to them. Your godly heritage must be thought through. Your kids are not going to automatically accept and pass down what you think that you are or have lived.
3.   Put your plan into action. A will is a document that is written down, signed by a notary, and carried out when the time is right. Your godly heritage must be put into action in everyday living. A godly heritage is lived out day after day after day. It is talked about, acted on and prayed over.

Will you live your life without making plans? I love the song, "I have a goodly heritage. I'm blessed with things you can't see. I have a goodly heritage. And that is worth far more to me."

Make plans today!

Pause to Ponder

Façade Blessings

Psalm 78:6-8
"That the generation to come might know them,
even the children which should be born; who should
arise and declare them to their children: That they
might set their hope in God, and not forget the works
of God, but keep his commandments: And might not be
as their fathers, a stubborn and rebellious generation;
a generation that set not their heart aright,
and whose spirit was not stedfast with God."

What do you think about when you think of the word *façade*? I think of something that is not totally what you think it is. You want it to look better than it really does so you add a fake front or you do things that cover what really is. The definition of *façade* is an outward appearance that is maintained to conceal a less pleasant or creditable reality.

What about the word *blessing*? The definition of *blessing* is God's favor and protection. The blessings of God on each of us are more than can be numbered. We are a blessed people. God's blessings come when we follow what He asks of us. God's blessings are real and nothing can take their place; however, we often façade the blessings of God. This happened in Psalm 78.

The 78th Psalm is so sad. There are 72 verses in this Psalm. Take a moment to read this sad, but true record of what God's people did. Verse 29 tells us that God's people had everything they desired, "So they did eat, and were well filled: for he gave them their own desire." God actually gave them their own desires. They were very lustful people. They didn't give up anything to follow God. While they were enjoying the desires of their hearts, the wrath of God came upon them. God's chosen people could have enjoyed and experienced the blessings of God, but instead, they followed their own lustful desires, thinking that they were truly receiving the blessings of God.

Remember that the desires of your heart cannot compare with the blessings of God. Remember who God is and that He knows who you are. "And they remembered that God was their rock, and the high God their redeemer. Nevertheless they did flatter him with their mouth, and they lied unto him with their tongues." (Ps. 78:35-36)

It's examination time!
1. Do you pray for desires and God gives them to you even though it's not His perfect will? (Ps. 78:29) God knows our stubbornness, and He knows the appetites of our heart.

2. Do you serve God but hold on to your fleshly appetites? (Ps. 78:30) Fleshly appetites are things that we put ahead of God in our everyday lives. It includes places we go, things we do, and the words that we speak. We enjoy these fleshly appetites, and we think that they are the blessings of God. However, they are not really the blessings of God. The fun and enjoyment we are experiencing is truly a façade.

3. Do you fear the judgment of God, or do you think

199

that you are exempt from it? We are living well, respected among our church family, have a good job, our family enjoys fun times, but we are not putting God in His rightful place.

Ask God to forgive you for living in the façade of His blessings. Asking God's forgiveness will put you in right standing with God, giving you a solid foundation to begin living in God's will, being "stedfast, unmovable, always abounding in the work of the Lord." (I Cor. 15:58)

"Being confident of this very thing, that he which hath begun a good work in you will perform it until the day of Jesus Christ." (Phil. 1:6) God will do His part. He will not quit or give up on you. The question is, will you choose a counterfeit life or a steadfast life? It's my prayer that you will not live well just because God gave you your own desire.

Pause to Ponder

Am I Limiting God?

Psalm 78:40-42
"How oft did they provoke him in the wilderness, and grieve him in the desert! Yea, they turned back and tempted God, and limited the Holy One of Israel. They remembered not his hand, nor the day when he delivered them from the enemy."

To limit simply means to restrict the ability to get the complete benefit of something; a restriction on the size or amount of something permissible or possible. A parent may limit a child's bread, soda or sweets. A teacher may limit the amount of recess time for her class. These are limits that are placed in our lives for the good. A speed limit is enforced for our safety, but today's verses speak of a different slant on limit. They refer to limiting God. God's people were limiting Him. They chose to live in a cycle of living for God, falling away from God, repenting to God and then repeat.

When God's people got punished, they would remember God. They remembered, but they didn't truly change. They tried to flatter God with their words. They lied to God. Their hearts were not right with God.

We are God's people. We follow the same cycle as the

children of Israel. We get into a situation which causes us to remember God. We repent and begin doing right. After a while, we fall back into our own selfish ways. We get into another situation, and we remember God…and the cycle continues.

Because of our selfish ways, we limit God. We are not happy or satisfied with our lives. We are not fulfilled in our desires. We are miserable, yet we continue to limit God due to our own selfish ways.

1. To remember God is not enough.
2. To flatter God is fooling yourself.
3. To lie to God is sin.
4. To be thoroughly right with God is where true blessing and happiness lies.
5. To be rooted and grounded in your faith is peace and joy!

None of us want to limit God, but all of us limit God in some way. What will I change in my life to not limit God?

Pause to Ponder

_____
_____
_____
_____
_____
_____
_____
_____
_____
_____
_____
_____
_____
_____
_____
_____
_____
_____
_____
_____
_____
_____
_____
_____
_____
_____

The Great Mystery

Ephesians 5:31-33
"For this cause shall a man leave his father
and mother, and shall be joined unto his wife,
and they two shall be one flesh. This is a great mystery:
but I speak concerning Christ and the church.
Nevertheless let every one of you in particular so love
his wife even as himself; and the wife see that
she reverence her husband."

Do you like a good mystery? They can be quite suspenseful. A mystery is something that is difficult or impossible to understand or explain. The husband/wife relationship is definitely one of those mysteries. The great mystery of marriage is compared to the great mystery of Christ and the church. How can a husband and wife become one flesh? We are two separate humans that have different personalities, likes and dislikes. A husband and wife should diligently work at their relationship, making it all that it should be. My husband and I are total opposites. You name it, and we do it differently. We are so opposite, yet we are the same. It's a mystery to me!

This mystery is resolved when we, as individuals, who care about our mate, prioritize our relationship with our mate. The mystery of Christ and the church is resolved when we, as the bride of Christ, conform to the image of His dear Son as stated in Romans 8:29, "For whom he did foreknow, he also did predestinate to be conformed to the image of his Son, that he might be the firstborn among many brethren."

1. Recognize that the husband/wife relationship is the primary relationship in the family. The parent/child relationship is important, yet secondary to this relationship. Recognize your relationship with Christ is the primary relationship in your Christian life. Your church family comes alongside you to support, love and influence you in a Christlike manner.

2. Strive to keep the fires burning in your relationship. (Eph. 5:22-24) Your marriage fire is ignited through proper attention, attitude, adjustments and adoration of each other. Your relationship with Christ is ignited through Bible reading, prayer, proper friendships and doing what you know to do is right.

3. Realize that your role as a submissive wife is indispensable. All three parts of the traditional family will suffer if you do not follow your role. Be submissive to your own husband. In Ephesians 5:22-24, the Bible speaks of submission as a functional lining up. Someone must be in charge. God designed the man for that role. See yourself on your husband's team and not as his opponent. Offer ideas, opinions and insights. Then, when your team leader (husband) makes his decision, support it because you are on the team!

4. Make a choice to align yourself with the will of your husband. Anticipate his desires; then, act in accordance with those desires.

5. Admire your husband. Admiration attracts. Belittling repels.

6. Look for opportunities to draw attention to his positive qualities. Compliment and praise him both privately and publicly.

7. Show appreciation for your husband's accomplishments in his job. Learn to accurately give his job description.

8. Be considerate of your husband's words. Think before responding.

9. Exercise your power of influence. As a wife, you have this power. Most of the time people with positions of influence have more power than people with positions of authority. It's been said that "the hand that rocks the cradle rules the world."

You possess the influence to make your marriage all God intended for it to be. Are the fires of romance still burning in your marriage? The fire must be stirred daily. Be a part of this great mystery!

Pause to Ponder

Thrive in Drive

Galatians 4:9
"But now, after that ye have known God,
or rather are known of God, how turn ye again
to the weak and beggarly elements, whereunto ye
desire again to be in bondage?"

Galatians 4 is an enlightening chapter. It makes me wonder, "Why do I want to be in bondage to negative thoughts? Why do I want to live worried, afraid, and heavy, when I can release it all and live free, excited, and joyful?"

I have no answer to my own why's except that I want my own way even if it is miserable. What freedom! I get my own way! WooHoo! No, it is true bondage! It is bondage to self which is sin instead of freedom in the spirit. This freedom in Christ is taken so wrong. I don't believe it means that I'm saved and free so I can live like I want to. That is going back to bondage but under a different disguise.

Galatians 4:9 calls it "weak and beggarly elements" which will eventually put you back into bondage. You and I have a choice to let go of the weak and beggarly elements in our lives.

Acting in accordance with the weak and beggarly elements in your life causes a lack of spiritual growth. The lack of spiritual growth causes the flesh to override the spirit. Fleshly living leads you to be critical of the spiritual things that once made you thrive. An example of freedom that is slavery is someone who goes to jail for a crime due to drugs and alcohol. They serve their time and get out of jail, only to have the cycle repeat itself. At this point, freedom becomes slavery. The weak and beggarly elements have become the ruling judgments in a person's life.

For our body and brain to be clear, we must have proper rest and think time. For lack of a better term, I will call it A-time. *A* equals amusement. Amusement means no thinking. Sometimes you need A-time. No thinking; just rest! Then, the clarity of thought will return to you. Delving into your Bible daily along with proper communication with God will help you to grow in the Christian life, causing you to overcome the weak and beggarly elements that come into your life.

We shouldn't live in overdrive, and we shouldn't live in neutral. Neither are good all of the time. We will hit those two areas occasionally; however, drive is where we should live. Drive is the balance! Thrive in drive to avoid the weak and beggarly elements that tempt you!

Pause to Ponder

_____
_____
_____
_____
_____
_____
_____
_____
_____
_____
_____
_____
_____
_____
_____
_____
_____
_____
_____
_____
_____
_____
_____
_____
_____
_____
_____

Day 58

Are You Thirsty?

Psalm 42:1
"As the hart panteth after the water brooks, so panteth
my soul after thee, O God."

Have you ever been so thirsty that you couldn't think about anything except how thirsty you were? When you are that thirsty, you just want water. Your body is craving it because it is calling out for a particular need; the need to be hydrated. When I am thirsty, I often try to satisfy my thirst for water with a substitute drink. Tea or soda tastes so yummy to me. They are a go-to treat, but the thirst factor remains. There is no substitute for the real thirst quencher–water!

In Psalm 42, the psalmist is thirsty. He is not physically thirsty, but instead, spiritually thirsty. The phrase in verse 1, "so panteth my soul after thee, O God" paints a portrait of the psalmist begging God to come and fill his thirsty need. He couldn't eat or sleep he was so spiritually thirsty. He prays; he remembers; he asks God questions.

Have you ever felt like God wasn't there? Like He didn't hear you? Just like the psalmist, your soul begs for the living God to reveal Himself. I will admit to you that I have had these feelings. We know He is there because God's

212

Word says so, but we don't feel His presence.

1.   When God is silent, it does not mean that He is absent.

2.   When your soul is in turmoil, sometimes it is something that you have caused, and God is simply waiting on you to repent.

3.   It is okay to ask God questions, but it is not okay to question God's integrity and authority.

4.   Remember that every answer to every question is found in God's Word.

5.   Stop trying to quench your spiritual thirst with a substitute of serving.

This psalmist closes with verse 11, "Why art thou cast down, O my soul? and why art thou disquieted within me? hope thou in God: for I shall yet praise him, who is the health of my countenance, and my God."

Are you thirsty? Put your hope in God, praise Him for He is: the health of your countenance!

Pause to Ponder

Day 59

Rich Feels Good

Proverbs 13:7
"There is that maketh himself rich, yet hath nothing:
there is that maketh himself poor, yet hath great riches."

As a child, I remember looking at a particular house and thinking that family was rich. That seemed like such a perfect lifestyle. I recall asking my mom for a store-bought birthday cake because I thought that was really special. I was enamored with name brands in my older youth because I didn't have it growing up, and it sounded so nice! I look back and wonder, "What was I thinking?" Simply, rich feels good.

Rich according to God's standards has nothing to do with this world's temporary satisfactions. There is nothing wrong with having nice things as long as they don't take first place in our lives. When we think highly of status and possessions in our lives, Christ is not first place. Often we think He is, but we don't show it through how we live. Rich feels good! Very good! God's Word explains simply how I can be rich.

1.   Put yourself in the proper place. "But many that are first shall be last; and the last shall be first." (Matt. 19:30)

2. Use your talents for God. "Then Peter said, Silver and gold have I none; but such as I have give I thee: In the name of Jesus Christ of Nazareth rise up and walk." (Acts 3:6)

3. Be teachable. "Receive my instruction, and not silver; and knowledge rather than choice gold." (Prov. 8:10) "For wisdom is better than rubies; and all the things that may be desired are not to be compared to it." (Prov. 8:11)

I am rich, and rich is good!

Pause to Ponder

My Lying Heart

I John 3:20
"For if our heart condemn us, God is greater than our heart, and knoweth all things."

Have you ever believed a lie, and, then, when you found out the truth, you just couldn't believe it? How can someone actually look another person in the eyes and tell them a lie? Lying is a sin, and it has been around since the beginning of time. The serpent lied to Eve, and there are many other lies recorded in the Bible. It is human nature to try to make yourself look better by enhancing a story.

I will always remember the first time that Philip, our middle son, told us a lie. He was in the 2nd grade. The class was involved in a reading challenge. Philip loved to read so much that reading was getting tiresome to him. He wanted to earn the reward of a free Personal Pan Pizza from Pizza Hut by reading a certain number of books. This particular week he lied to us about reading all of the books. I questioned his reading because we had just gone to the library and checked out a bunch of books. I knew it was impossible for him to have read that many books in a couple of days. When we asked him about reading all of the books, he admitted that he had lied. I remember being disappointed, hurt, and afraid that he would develop the habit of lying. One of my favorite books to illustrate lying was and still is *The Berenstain Bears and the Truth*. The story deals with how lying develops a lack of trust once you have lied, and trust is something that is difficult to put back together once it is broken.

Your heart regularly lies to you. The first lie is that you are not worthy to be loved. This is a lie straight from the devil. No matter your background, history, or social status, you are worthy to be loved by God and others. The second lie is God can't use me. The third lie is I'm not gifted with anything to do for God. The fourth lie is that no one cares.

The story is told of the Old Nature and the New Nature. We are born with the Old Nature. The Old Nature has a sinful, lying heart. When we get saved, the New Nature moves in. We now have two natures. This is like 2 dogs in a fight that live inside of us. The one that wins each battle is the one we feed the most.

"And the peace of God, which passeth all understanding, shall keep your hearts and minds through Christ Jesus." (Phil. 4:7)

You and I have a lying heart. Ask yourself, "What lies is my heart telling me?"

Pause to Ponder